£7.99

CHAMPIONS OF EUROPE

ED BOY IS SIR'S HERO!

EDWIN VAN DER SAR
POSITION: Keeper
BORN: October 29, 1970, Voorout, Netherlands
HEIGHT: 1.98m (6ft 6in)
PREVIOUS CLUBS: Ajax, Juventus, Fulham
DID YOU KNOW? Edwin was in goal when Ajax beat AC Milan 1-0 in the 1995 Champions League Final. The following year his Amsterdam side lost a penalty shoot-out in the final against Juventus.

MANCHESTER UNITED became the Champions of Europe for a third time thanks to Sir Alex Ferguson's "Ed Boy".

Holland keeper Edwin van der Sar pulled off a dramatic penalty shoot-out save from Chelsea's Nicolas Anelka to ensure Champions League victory for the Red Devils.

After the Moscow showdown between the Premier League's top two sides had ended 1-1 after normal and extra time, the drama of penalties decided the outcome of the continent's biggest club prize.

Inevitably, red-hot Cristiano Ronaldo had put United ahead and it was the battling Frank Lampard who equalised just before half time.

United had dominated the first half but there was no question the Blues battled better in the second 45 minutes.

As the rain lashed down in Russia, Didier Drogba, who had earlier hit the post, was sent off in the dying stages of extra time for slapping Nemanja Vidic and the Londoners had lost one of their spot-kick takers.

Double Footballer of the Year Ronaldo was crestfallen after missing his penalty but Chelsea skipper John Terry was inconsolable when he failed to bury the kick that would have given his side the trophy. He spent the next 24 hours crying over his failure.

When Anelka's spot kick was dramatically saved by van der Sar it was all over and Fergie had collected his second European Cup.

THE SHOOT-OUT

Man United 6 Chelsea 5

Tevez ✔	Ballack ✔
Carrick ✔	Belletti ✔
Ronaldo ✗	Lampard ✔
Hargreaves ✔	A. Cole ✔
Nani ✔	Terry ✗
Anderson ✔	Kalou ✔
Giggs ✔	Anelka ✗

UNITED FRONT!

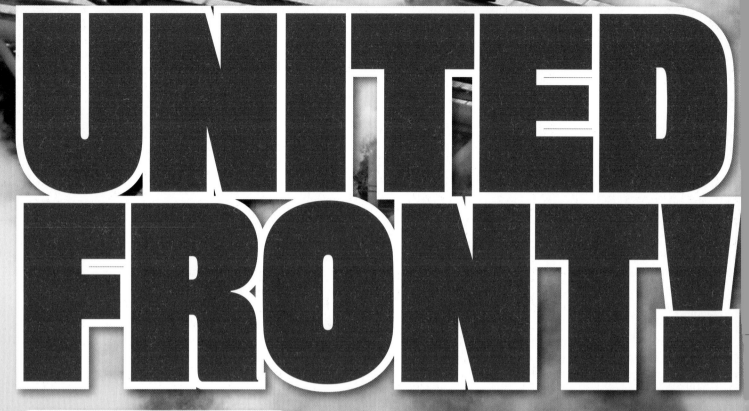

FINAL COUNTDOWN

2007-08	P	W	D	L	F	A	GD	PTS
Man United	38	27	6	5	80	22	58	87
Chelsea	38	25	10	3	65	26	39	85
Arsenal	38	24	11	3	74	31	34	83
Liverpool	38	21	13	4	67	28	39	76

10 FROM 16 FOR FERGIE'S BOYS

THEY STARTED THE season in rubbish form but Sir Alex Ferguson can always be relied on to sort out the problems!

After drawing against Reading and Portsmouth and losing at bitter rivals Man City, in their first three games, few expected Manchester United to lift the Premier League title for the TENTH time in 16 seasons at the end of 2007-08.

Fergie had brought in the relatively unheard of Nani and Anderson to boost his campaign, along with the often underrated Owen Hargreaves.

Argentina striker Carlos Tevez was added up front but the pundits still reckoned the Red Devils would have a big job defending their title.

But a young Portuguese winger had different ideas! Cristiano Ronaldo bagged 31 Premiership goals in as many starts making him United's highest scoring wide man ever! He beat the 40-year-old record set by George Best.

Tevez, Wayne Rooney and Ronaldo combined to net 57 goals. United leaked the least number of goals of any Premiership side – 22 – whilst crashing 80 into the back of the net.

After their dismal start, Man United got their season quickly back on track and their 1-0 victory over Liverpool on December 15, 2007 signalled the start of a massive push for yet more glory.

Now, with a further season's experience under their belts, it will take something special to rob the Old Trafford stars of the title by the end of 2008-09.

Even though the title race went to the very last game of the campaign, very few doubted that United would beat Wigan on the final day.

Chelsea had to get a better result than United in their last game to be crowned Champions. But Fergie's boys confidently flew past Wigan 2-0 and Chelsea were held to a draw by Bolton at Stamford Bridge, as their late bid for glory fizzled out.

CHAMPION'S FACTS 07-08

TOP SCORER: Cristiano Ronaldo 31
HIGHEST CROWD: 76,013 v West Ham
LOWEST CROWD: 75,055 v Fulham
CLEAN SHEETS: 21
BLANKS: 3
DOUBLES ACHIEVED: 9 (Aston Villa, Birmingham City, Derby County, Everton, Fulham, Liverpool, Newcastle, Sunderland, Wigan)
DOUBLES SUFFERED: 1 (Man City)
KEY WIN: Beating Wigan 2-0
WORST RESULT: 2-1 home defeat to Man City
HAT-TRICKS: 1 (Ronaldo v Newcastle)
NUMBER OF GOALSCORERS: 13
PLAYERS USED: 25
BAD LADS: Wayne Rooney and Wes Brown, both had eight yellow cards.

WHO'S WON WHEN UNITED HAVEN'T!

Blackburn 1995
Arsenal 1998, 2002, 2004
Chelsea 2005, 2006

COMPLIMENTS OF THE SEASON

WHO WON WHAT IN 2007-08

WEST BROMWICH ALBION

CHAMPIONSHIP CHAMPIONS

The Baggies bounced back to the Premier League following a two-year absence after boss Tony Mowbray's first full season in charge. His side had been beaten in the previous year's play-off final by Derby.
ALSO PROMOTED: Stoke City, Hull City.

CHAMPIONS 2008
SWANSEA CITY F.C.

SWANSEA CITY

LEAGUE ONE CHAMPIONS

Just 14 months after taking over as boss at the Liberty Stadium, Roberto Martinez helped the Swans glide back into the second tier of English football. It's the first time in 24 years that the Welshmen have been this high in the leagues. The success earned Martinez, a former midfielder at City, a new contract and the League One Manager of the Year award.
ALSO PROMOTED: Nottingham Forest, Doncaster.

MK DONS

LEAGUE TWO CHAMPIONS

Former England captain Paul Ince's first season in charge saw the Dons take the title. Danny Swailes, Dean Lewington, Keith Andrews and Lloyd Dyer were all named in the PFA's League Two Team of the Year.
ALSO PROMOTED: Peterborough, Hereford, Stockport.

CELTIC

SCOTTISH PREMIER LEAGUE

Just like its English counterpart, the SPL went to the last game of the season and could have been settled on goal difference. But Rangers lost 2-0 at Aberdeen and Celtic snatched a 1-0 victory at Dundee United to take the title by three points.

Clydesdale Bank
PREMIER LEAGUE CHAMPIONS 07-08

Clydesdale Bank PREMIER LEAGUE
CHAMPIONS 07-08

ALDERSHOT TOWN

BLUE SQUARE PREMIER CHAMPIONS

The Shots returned to league football 16 years after they were forced to start all over again because of a cash crisis.
ALSO PROMOTED: Exeter City.

WINNERS 2008

RANGERS
SCOTTISH CUP

The blue half of Glasgow had hoped this fixture would give them a quadruple of trophies (with the UEFA Cup, CIS Cup and SPL). But in the end it completed a domestic cups double. Rangers took a two goal lead against Queen of the South but were pegged back to 2-2 before Kris Boyd got his second of the game to make it 3-2.

SCOTTISH CUP WINNERS 2008

PORTSMOUTH
FA CUP

Pompey lifted the famous trophy for the first time in 69 years thanks to a first-half goal against Cardiff from Kanu. The Nigeria striker had already collected two FA Cup winner's medals during his time at Arsenal.

RANGERS
CIS CUP

Rangers were twice down but bounced back to level the scores at 2-2 after extra-time. They then won the penalty shoot-out against Dundee United 3-2.

MK DONS
JOHNSTONE'S PAINT TROPHY

It was Paul Ince's first trophy as a manager and the club's first silverware since changing from Wimbledon. Their 2-0 win over Grimsby came with goals from Keith Andrews and Sean O'Hanlon.

CARLING CUP

TOTTENHAM
CARLING CUP

Spurs won their first trophy since 1999 when they beat London rivals Chelsea thanks to an extra time winner from Jonathan Woodgate. It was the defender's first goal after moving from Middlesbrough. Didier Drogba put Chelsea ahead before Dimitar Berbatov's penalty equaliser.

EBBSFLEET UNITED
THE FA TROPHY

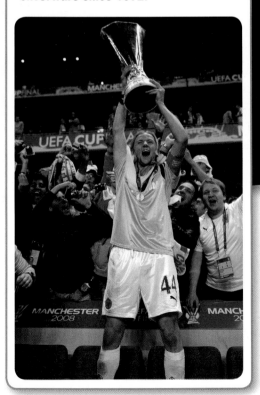

Chris McPhee had a penalty saved and then scored the only goal as Ebbsfleet United beat Torquay at Wembley in front of 40,000 fans. United had been taken over earlier in the season when 20,000 supporters paid £35 each for a share in the club.

KIRKHAM AND WESHAM
THE FA VASE

Teenage substitute Matt Walwyn hit two as Lancashire side Kirkham and Wesham came back from 1-0 down against Lowestoft Town at Wembley to win 2-1.

ZENIT ST. PETERSBURG
UEFA CUP

Two goals in the last 20 minutes at the City of Manchester Stadium saw Zenit St. Petersburg deny Rangers a chance of lifting their first European silverware since 1972.

CRISTIANO RONALDO
PFA AND FOOTBALLER WRITERS' PLAYER OF THE YEAR

Ronnie became only the second player to collect both these awards in successive seasons. The last star to achieve this feat was Thierry Henry during his time at Arsenal in 2003 and 2004.

CESC FABREGAS
PFA YOUNG PLAYER OF THE YEAR

Arsenal's sensational Spain midfielder picked up the award that Cristiano Ronaldo had won the previous campaign. He dedicated the victory to his team mates.

10 THINGS YOU NEED TO KNOW ABOUT... CESC FABREGAS

1 Spain sensation Francesc "Cesc" Fabregas Soler was born on May 4, 1987, in Arenys de Mar, just along the coast from his first club – Barcelona.

2 He became Arsenal's youngest-ever first-team player when he made his debut against Rotherham in the League Cup at the age of 16 years and 177 days. Five weeks later he became their youngest-ever scorer with a strike against Wolves.

3 Cesc starred in his very own TV programme during 2008 – *The Cesc Fabregas Show* on Sky Sports! As well as top football stars, the show featured *Little Britain* funnyman Matt Lucas.

7 At 19, Cesc was the youngest-ever footballer to play in a World Cup for Spain. He featured in each of the group games in Germany in 2006, and played the full 90 minutes in his country's 3-1 defeat against France in the second round.

4 The central midfielder won the PFA Young Player of the Year award in 2008. The modest star dedicated the win to his fellow Arsenal players. "Without them I would not have won," he said.

8 His childhood hero was Josep Guardiola (right), a member of the fantastic Barcelona side of the early 1990s. Guardiola also wore the number 4 shirt.

9 He can speak Spanish, English and a bit of French – useful in a conversation with Arsenal team-mates Manuel Almunia, Theo Walcott and William Gallas!

5 His goalscoring ability was easy to spot at a very early age. Not only was he named Player of the Tournament at the 2003 FIFA Under-17 World Championship – he picked up the Golden Boot as top scorer too!

10 Fabregas has earned praise from the best in the game. Liverpool skipper Steven Gerrard said: "The world is his oyster. He can go on to be one of the best in the world."

6 Fabregas wears the number 4 shirt. Other famous Arsenal number 4s include Gunners' legends Frank McLintock and Patrick Vieira.

CESC FABREGAS

ONES TO WATCH!

We reveal the young stars who are aiming to be the megastars of tomorrow

VICTOR MOSES

BORN: December 12, 1990, Lagos, Nigeria
CLUB: Crystal Palace
NATIONALITY: English
HEIGHT: 1.77m (5ft 10in)
WEIGHT: 75 kg (11st 12lb)
WHAT'S HIS GAME? Powerful centre forward or winger with a bullet shot. Former Selhurst colleague Clinton Morrison admits: "The things that he can do on the training pitch are unbelievable. He has a lot of talent and really has got it all."

RAY PUTTERILL

BORN: March 2, 1989, Liverpool
CLUB: Liverpool
NATIONALITY: English
HEIGHT: 1.72m (5ft 8in)
WEIGHT: 77.6kg (12st 3lb)
WHAT'S HIS GAME? Left-sided midfielder who can score goals. Has represented England Under-16s.

JAY SIMPSON
BORN: December 27, 1988, London
CLUB: Arsenal
NATIONALITY: English
HEIGHT: 1.80m (5ft 11in)
WEIGHT: 84.4kg (13st 4lb)
WHAT'S HIS GAME? Striker or winger. First player to score a hat-trick at the Emirates Stadium. Under-18 debut for Arsenal at 13. On loan at Millwall, he was League 1 Player of the Season.

NATHAN PORRITT
BORN: January 19, 1990, Middlesbrough
CLUB: Middlesbrough
NATIONALITY: English
HEIGHT: 1.76m (5ft 9in)
WEIGHT: 74.8kg (11st 10lb)
WHAT'S HIS GAME? Without even making his first team debut, the midfielder had attracted the attention of a host of big name clubs. England Under-18 player.

KAZENGA LUA LUA
BORN: December 10, 1990, Kinshasa, DR Congo
CLUB: Newcastle
NATIONALITY: Congolese
HEIGHT: 1.80m (5ft 11in)
WEIGHT: 76kg (12st)
WHAT'S HIS GAME? This tricky midfielder is the younger brother of former Newcastle and Portsmouth hitman Lomana Lua Lua. Bags of skill and speed and predicted to break through soon.

BEN MEE
CLUB: Manchester City
NATIONALITY: English
WHAT'S HIS GAME: Mee was skipper of last season's FA Youth Cup-winning side and voted the club's most promising player. It was the first time the club had won the trophy in 22 years and earned the defender a place in the senior squad. He got an international call up from England for last summer's Under-19 European Championships in the Czech Republic.

RYAN BERTRAND
BORN: August 5, 1989, Southwark, London
CLUB: Chelsea
NATIONALITY: English
HEIGHT: 1.78m (5ft 10in)
WEIGHT: 69.8kg (11st)
WHAT'S HIS GAME? He's a left-winger or left-back who spent a lot of last season on loan at Norwich. Bought from Gillingham for £125,000 as a 16-year-old, he has played for England Under-17s and 19s.

FRED SEARS
BORN: November 27, 1989, Hornchurch, Essex
CLUB: West Ham
NATIONALITY: English
HEIGHT: 1.71m (5ft 7in)
WEIGHT: 75kg (11st 11lb)
WHAT'S HIS GAME? The England Under-19 star is a tricky, nippy striker who gets behind defenders and can unleash wicked shots.

DAN GOSLING
BORN: February 2, 1990, Brixham, Devon
CLUB: Everton
NATIONALITY: English
HEIGHT: 1.78m (5ft 10in)
WEIGHT: 71.3kg (11st 3lb)
WHAT'S HIS GAME? The right-back can also play as a holding midfielder and was on Chelsea's shopping list before Everton swooped in January 2008 for £1m, rising to £2m. England Under-17 and Under-18.

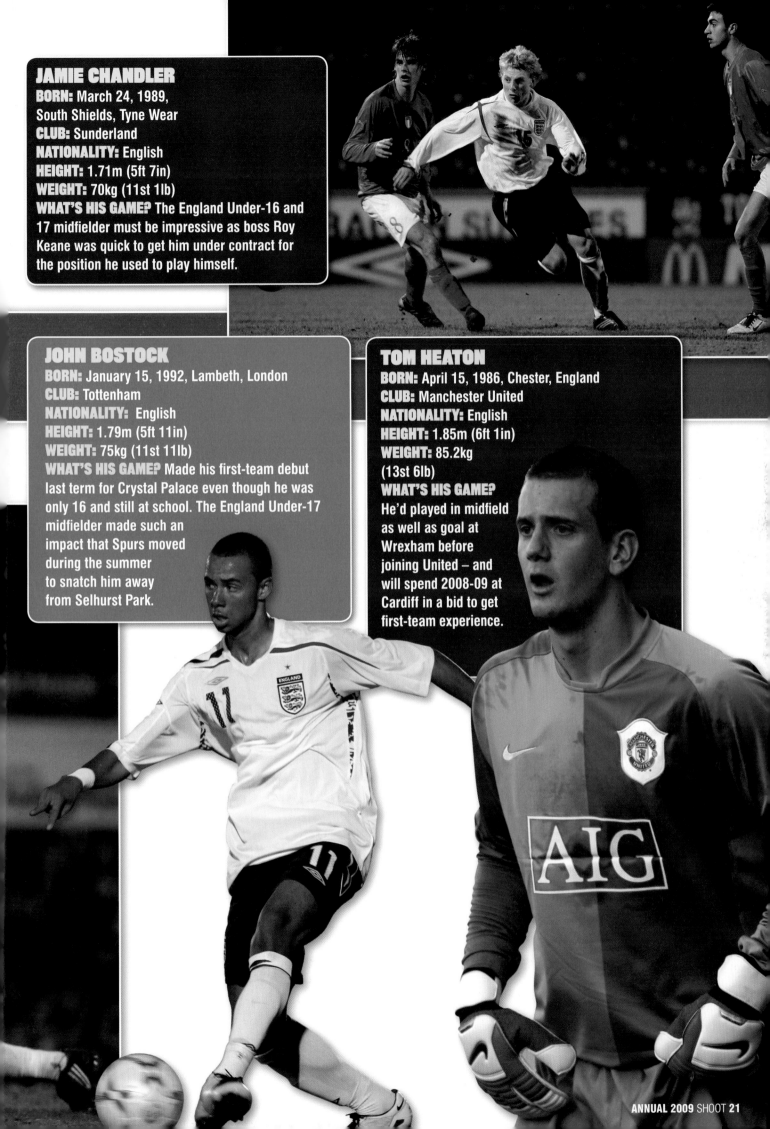

JAMIE CHANDLER

BORN: March 24, 1989, South Shields, Tyne Wear
CLUB: Sunderland
NATIONALITY: English
HEIGHT: 1.71m (5ft 7in)
WEIGHT: 70kg (11st 1lb)
WHAT'S HIS GAME? The England Under-16 and 17 midfielder must be impressive as boss Roy Keane was quick to get him under contract for the position he used to play himself.

JOHN BOSTOCK

BORN: January 15, 1992, Lambeth, London
CLUB: Tottenham
NATIONALITY: English
HEIGHT: 1.79m (5ft 11in)
WEIGHT: 75kg (11st 11lb)
WHAT'S HIS GAME? Made his first-team debut last term for Crystal Palace even though he was only 16 and still at school. The England Under-17 midfielder made such an impact that Spurs moved during the summer to snatch him away from Selhurst Park.

TOM HEATON

BORN: April 15, 1986, Chester, England
CLUB: Manchester United
NATIONALITY: English
HEIGHT: 1.85m (6ft 1in)
WEIGHT: 85.2kg (13st 6lb)
WHAT'S HIS GAME? He'd played in midfield as well as goal at Wrexham before joining United – and will spend 2008-09 at Cardiff in a bid to get first-team experience.

PREMIERSHIP
SECRETS

STUNNING FACTS ABOUT STAR PLAYERS – INCLUDING STUFF THEY MAY NOT WANT YOU TO KNOW!

G-WHIZ!

STEVEN GERRARD is becoming a property tycoon! The England midfielder is rapidly rivalling former Liverpool team mate Robbie Fowler in the house-buying stakes. Stevie G already lives with his family in a massive mansion in his home city and has a luxury flat in the French Alps plus a villa on the sunny Algarve. But he has also invested around £4.5m in three penthouses right by the Mersey and close to the famous Liver Building. He has agreed the deal as he tries to safeguard the financial future of his family.

MAMA MIA

MAMADY SIDIBE'S chance of making his Premier League debut was nearly taken away from him after he was stabbed by a crazed fan!

The Mali striker hit the two goals that helped Stoke City to promotion and was carried off the pitch on fans' shoulders. But when he helped his country put Togo out of the African Cup of Nations he was punched out cold, then knifed and had to flee from a riot!

The 6ft 4in hitman had to undergo two hours of surgery... but only after his ambulance had been stoned on its way to hospital.

BULLY, BULLY

Mad midfielder **JIMMY BULLARD** loves his golf, fishing, football... and music that his team-mates think is outdated.

The Fulham battler reckons nothing gets you fired up for a game better than a blast from veteran rockers Status Quo!

"I'm not having any of the R 'n' B rubbish – how are you meant to get up for a game with that?" asked the likeable East Ender.

TAKING THE MICHAEL

MICHAEL BALLACK FANCIES himself as a bit of an actor.

The Chelsea and Germany midfielder has appeared in adverts for McDonalds and flash car makers Mercedes.

His latest car ad saw him stick on a fake moustache so that he looked like intrepid adventurer Indiana Jones!

STICK IT TO 'EM!

DEAN KIELY helped West Brom bounce back into the Premiership and then proved he is as good with the sticks as he is between them!

The Baggies' former Republic of Ireland keeper won the Goalkeepers Cup at a golf day in Kent, no mean feat when you consider a lot of players like a day on the greens.

And talking of greens, fellow shot-stopper Rob Green spent most of his holidays raising cash for his Africa-based charity, a task that included marching up Mount Kilimanjaro.

WHO ARE YOU?

Newcastle and Nigeria striker **OBAFEMI MARTINS** admits he had to find out about boss Kevin Keegan by watching YouTube!

The tricky hitman was away on African Nations duty when Special K took over at St. James' Park but he wanted to find out if the legendary stories about KK were true.

"I went to YouTube because I wanted to see for myself what he was like as a player and how the team played when he was last here," admitted Oba.

"The team that came so close to the title when he was here last time was a great team. No wonder they were called The Entertainers."

WHERE TO NOW?

Middlesbrough and France forward **JEREMIE ALIADIERE** is running out of skin! The former Arsenal striker isn't quite sure where he can fit in his next tattoo.

He's got a barcode inked on one wrist with his mum's and dad's dates of birth and on the other he has his gran's birthdate and when she died.

There's also a small star and angel wings on his back. Wonder if that's where he gets his speed!

A to Z of... FOOTBALL NICKNAMES

A

AZZURRI
How the Italian fans refer to their national side because they play in an azure shade of blue. Current champions Italy have won the World Cup four times in total.

b

BIG AL
Newcastle United's legendary Geordie striker Alan Shearer is affectionately known by the Toon Army as "Big Al". The former England captain is the Premier League's all-time top scorer with 260 goals.

C

CARRA
Liverpool's committed centre back Jamie Carragher is known as "Carra" by his team-mates and Reds fans, although many of the Anfield faithful would christen him the "King of the Kop".

D

DIEU
"Dieu", which is French for God, is what the Manchester United fans labelled Gallic genius Eric Cantona during the 1990s. The flair-filled striker was also known as "The King" and won four Premier League titles during his time at Old Trafford. Another former United striker, Denis Law, was also known as "The King".

EL TEL
How the media referred to Terry Venables when he coached Spanish giants Barcelona in the 1980s. The nickname stuck and the former England coach is still often called "El Tel". During his time with Barca, Venables won the Spanish League title and guided the Catalan side to the European Cup Final where they lost to Romanian champions Steaua Bucharest.

FOXES
The nickname for League One side Leicester City as Leicestershire used to be known for foxes and hunting. A former Premiership side, the Foxes have won the League Cup twice in the last ten years and can boast England legends Gordon Banks, Peter Shilton and Gary Lineker as former players.

GAZZA
One of the most talented English footballers ever, Paul Gascoigne has been affectionately known as "Gazza" by team mates, fans and the media for most of his life. The Geordie gem was also labelled "The Clown Prince" due to his love for practical jokes and wind-ups.

HORSE
Former Arsenal and Dynamo Kiev right-back Oleg Luzhny was known as the "Horse" due to awesome energy levels and electrifying pace. Former Liverpool and England captain Emlyn Hughes was famously christened "Crazy Horse" by legendary ex-Anfield boss Bill Shankly in the 1970s.

IRONS
As well as the "Hammers", West Ham are also known as the "Irons". This name refers back to the club's previous name when they were formed as Thames Ironworks FC in 1895. They became West Ham five years later.

JT
Chelsea and England's inspirational defender John Terry is better known by his initials. The Blues captain has won two Premier League titles, two League Cups and an FA Cup in recent years.

KING KENNY
Liverpool supporters' name for legendary former striker Kenny Dalglish who starred for the Reds in the 1980s. The skilful Scot was known as "King Kenny" or the "King of the Kop". Dalglish enjoyed success both as a player and manager of the Merseyside giants.

LES BLEUS
What French fans call their national side. "Les Bleus" translates to "The Blues" and is often heard in the famous chant "Allez Les Bleus", which means "Go The Blues".

A to Z of... FOOTBALL NICKNAMES

NIJINSKY

One of Manchester City's finest players, central midfielder Colin Bell, was dubbed Nijinsky after the famous racehorse. Bell earned the nickname due to his all-action, energetic displays and as far as City fans are concerned he certainly was a footballing thoroughbred. The former England star was also known as "The King of the Kippax" which was the home stand at City's old Maine Road ground.

N

MAGPIES

The nickname of Premiership side Newcastle United, referring to their distinctive black and white striped shirts. The North East club have played in the Premier League since 1993.

m

OWLS

The nickname of current Championship side Sheffield Wednesday. The Owls played in the Premier League from 1992 to 2000 and often finished in the top half. Some of their star players during the 1990s were Chris Waddle, Des Walker and David Hirst. Wednesday are known as the Owls because their home ground, Hillsborough, is in Owlerton.

POMPEY

How Premiership side Portsmouth are better known, originally by their local fans, and now all over England. The South Coast club's famous terrace chant is "Play up Pompey, Pompey play up", and they certainly have been in recent seasons under the guidance of manager Harry Redknapp.

P

o

r

SICKNOTE

Former Spurs and England midfielder Darren Anderton was cruelly dubbed "Sicknote" by the English media due to the injuries he suffered and the number of games he missed. Despite the label, Anderton, also referred to as "Shaggy" due to his resemblance to the Scooby Doo cartoon character, actually played 30 times for England and scored nine goals. Darren has recently been playing for Bournemouth.

Q

QUAKERS

The nickname of League Two side Darlington, it refers to the religious movement of the same name which historically had an influence on the town. They are also known as "Darlo".

RED DEVILS

The famous nickname of English giants and current Premiership champions Manchester United. The "Red Devils" was adopted in the 1960s and is taken from the nickname of the nearby Salford Reds Rugby League team.

S

TOFFEES

The shortened version of Premier League side Everton's nickname "The Toffeemen". There are a number of explanations of how the name came about, including the location of a toffee shop near the ground, a house called "ye olde toffee house", also nearby, or because the word "toffee" was slang for Irishmen, many of whom used to live and work in Liverpool and supported the side.

U

UNTOUCHABLES

When Arsenal won the 2003-04 Premiership title they went unbeaten for the entire 38-game season and were labelled the "Untouchables". When Preston North End achieved the same feat in 1888-89 – as well as claiming the FA Cup – they were called the "Invincibles".

T

VILLANS

Surprisingly not the nickname for any criminals at all – but that of Premier League Aston Villa. It refers to the "Villa" part of their name.

V

W

WAZZA

One of the pet names given to Manchester United and England star striker Wayne Rooney. Others include "The Roon", "The Roonster" and "Roonaldo".

X

XAVI

The shortened name of Barcelona's midfield ace Xavier Hernandez Creus. The Spain international is one of the more underrated stars of Barca's great team but is vital to the way the Catalans play.

YORKIE

How current Sunderland striker Dwight Yorke is addressed by his team mates. But unlike the chocolate bar of the same name, the Trinidad and Tobago treble winner is seemingly for girls!

Y

ZIZOU

One of the greatest players of the modern era, former France star Zinedine Zidane was known by the French press and public as "Zizou". The ex-Real Madrid and Juventus legend won the World Cup, European Championships and Champions League medals during his amazing career.

Z

WHO DO THEY REALLY SUPPORT?

WE GOT SOME STAR PLAYERS TO ADMIT THEY DON'T PLAY FOR THEIR FAVOURITE TEAMS...

LINVOY PRIMUS
PORTSMOUTH
WEST HAM

"I supported Tottenham when I was younger but tended to watch West Ham as it was nearer."

MICHAEL OWEN
NEWCASTLE
EVERTON

"I supported Everton as a kid and they are a great club. But it's great to score in the Merseyside derby!"

DAVID BENTLEY
BLACKBURN
ARSENAL

"Although I watched Arsenal since I was 12, I followed players instead of supporting a team. I looked up to Dennis Bergkamp after seeing him at close quarters."

MICAH RICHARDS
MAN CITY
ARSENAL

"I supported Arsenal when I was growing up and I admired Patrick Vieira. I liked Roy Keane as well as they were both good leaders."

THEO WALCOTT
ARSENAL
LIVERPOOL

"Liverpool. I inherited my alliance from my father Don who is a lifetime Liverpool supporter."

ROBBIE KEANE
TOTTENHAM
CELTIC

"Everyone wants to be Brazil when they play as a youngster, but I'm a Celtic fan, and I have said that one day I would like to play for them."

JAMIE CARRAGHER
LIVERPOOL
EVERTON

"I was an Everton fan but I wouldn't stop my son if he was good enough and wanted to play for Man United or Chelsea."

DIMITAR BERBATOV
TOTTENHAM
NEWCASTLE

"Newcastle. When I was young I really liked Marco van Basten and Alan Shearer. When we were playing and I got the ball I would say those names."

ASHLEY YOUNG
ASTON VILLA
ARSENAL

"I was a big Arsenal fan and Ian Wright was my hero. I still watch his videos today. Whenever I wasn't playing I would go to Highbury and was inspired to score goals."

IRON MAN!

Forget Superman, Spiderman and the rest of your superheroes. England and Chelsea defender **JOHN TERRY** leaves them all standing when it comes to bouncing back from injuries

HEAD

Knocked out stone cold in the Carling Cup Final he went to hospital – but was back in time for Chelsea's celebration party!

FACE

He should have been out of action for six weeks with a broken cheekbone. JT slapped on a protective mask and was playing again in just three days.

BACK

Slipped a disc. That's very painful – but John insisted on walking off the pitch and was back a week ahead of schedule.

KNEE
Back in action another seven days before he should have been after damaging medial ligaments.

HAMSTRING
Two weeks out instead of the usual eight. He's made of metal!

BROKEN FOOT
Back two weeks ahead of schedule after smashing three bones in his right foot.

BRAVE OR BONKERS?

You're right to think JT is as hard as nails, but don't forget these guys!

JASON ROBERTS
Played the last 80 minutes of a game with a broken leg to help Wigan win promotion to the Premiership.

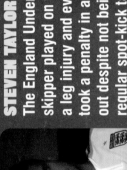

STEVEN TAYLOR
The England Under-21 skipper played on with a leg injury and even took a penalty in a shoot out despite not being a regular spot-kick taker.

TERRY BUTCHER
Who can forget his blood-spattered shirt and head bandage during qualification for Italia '90?

10 THINGS YOU NEED TO KNOW ABOUT FERNANDO TORRES

1 Fernando José Torres Sanz was born on March 20, 1984, in Fuenlabrada, a suburb of Madrid in Spain.

2 His nickname is "El Niño" – which means "The Kid" – because of his youthful appearance.

3 Torres scored three times during the 2006 World Cup in Germany – twice against Tunisia and once against Ukraine during the group stages.

4 He joined Atletico Madrid aged 11 after being spotted by their talent scouts. At 17 he became the youngest footballer to play for the Spanish legends and at 19 he was the youngest player to captain the side.

5 His reported £25m-plus signing was a transfer fee record for Liverpool, beating the £14m then-manager Gerard Houllier paid for striker Djibril Cisse in 2003-04

6 He scored 24 goals in the Premiership during 2007-08. That's a record for a foreign player during his first season in the Premier League.

7 On the inside of his left arm he has Fernando tattooed in "tengwar" – a language devised by JRR Tolkien, the author of *The Lord of the Rings*.

8 He plays in the number nine shirt, also worn by Kop legends Robbie Fowler and Ian Rush.

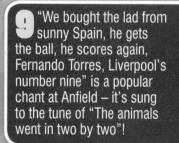

9 "We bought the lad from sunny Spain, he gets the ball, he scores again, Fernando Torres, Liverpool's number nine" is a popular chant at Anfield – it's sung to the tune of "The animals went in two by two"!

10 Before the start of the 2008-09 season Torres' number nine shirt was the most pre-ordered by Liverpool fans. Steven Gerrard's shirt was the second most popular and midfielder Javier Mascherano's third.

FERNANDO TORRES

WORDS OF WISDOM!

SOMETIMES FOOTBALLERS AND BOSSES SHOULD LEARN TO KEEP THEIR MOUTHS SHUT...

"I'M ALRIGHT IN THE CHANGING ROOMS BEFORE THE GAME BUT AS SOON AS I SIT IN MY SEAT AND THE MUSIC STARTS I JUST WANT TO GO HOME BECAUSE IT ANNOYS ME." BORO'S ANDREW TAYLOR IS NOT A GOOD FOOTBALL WATCHER WHILST INJURED

"ASHLEY WILL BE EVEN BETTER WHEN HE PUTS ON SOME WEIGHT. HE MUST BE THREE AND A HALF STONE NOW." MARTIN O'NEILL IS A BIT WORRIED ABOUT ASHLEY YOUNG'S ZERO FIGURE!

"ANYONE CAUGHT SMOKING WILL BE TAKEN TO A DARKENED ROOM WHERE THEY WILL BE IMPRISONED FOR 27 HOURS AND BE FORCED TO LISTEN TO WILL YOUNG RECORDS." THE COLCHESTER UNITED GROUND ANNOUNCER STANDS FOR NO NONSENSE

"I'VE GOT TO THE POINT WHERE I FEEL I HAVE TO SAVE THREE PENALTIES AND SCORE A GOAL TO HAVE A DECENT GAME."
PAUL ROBINSON LEARNS WHAT IT'S LIKE TO CARRY THE DODGY KEEPER TAG

"MY MISSUS GOES BONKERS SOMETIMES WHEN I COME BACK STINKING OF FISH. AND SHE GETS THE HUMP WHEN THE CAR'S ALL MUDDY. I DO STILL MAKE A PRAT OF MYSELF. I'VE FALLEN IN AND DROPPED MY PHONE IN THE LAKE."
JIMMY BULLARD CARPS ON ABOUT HOW HE'S HOOKED ON FISHING!

"HIS STRIKE RATE IN THE EARLY DAYS WAS DIABOLICAL, AND THAT'S BEING KIND TO HIM."
HARRY REDKNAPP ADMITS EX-POMPEY STRIKER BENJANI WASN'T PROLIFIC AT FRATTON PARK

OLLY DAYS....

THE SHOOT ANNUAL AND FOOTBALL JUST ISN'T THE SAME WITHOUT A FEW GREAT WORDS FROM IAN HOLLOWAY...

"I'M GETTING CALLS FROM AGENTS AROUND THE WORLD, PLAYERS WANT TO COME TO LEICESTER. I HAD TO BEAT 'EM UP, DRUG 'EM AND DRAG 'EM DOWN TO PLYMOUTH."

"FOOTBALL'S A SIMPLE GAME MADE COMPLICATED BY IDIOTS LIKE ME."

"APPARENTLY SIR ALEX FERGUSON WASN'T ALLOWED TO WATCH A COUPLE OF FRIENDLIES BECAUSE HIS WIFE WANTED HIM TO HELP MOVE HOUSE. GOOD JOB SHE DID, IF HE'D GONE ALONG TO THE GAMES HE WOULDN'T HAVE KNOWN WHERE HE'D MOVED TO, WOULD HE?"

"I CAN STILL GET IN MY 32s BUT I'VE GOT A BIT OF AN EDDIE KELLY [BELLY, ED] COMING OVER THE TOP. IT LOOKS LIKE I'VE GOT A MICHELIN MAN GROWING THERE. I HATE TO SAY IT BUT I'M GETTING MIDDLE-AGED."

"WHEN WE SHARE A ROOM HE HAS TO WAKE UP 20 MINUTES BEFORE ME BECAUSE HE HAS TO DO HIS HAIR AND APPLY HIS FACE CREAMS."
MIKEL ARTETA REVEALS EVERTON TEAM-MATE TIM CAHILL ISN'T THE HARD AUSSIE HE CLAIMS!

GIANT CROSSWORD

You can check out the answers on page 110 – but not until you have finished the questions.

CLUES ACROSS

1 The - - -, home of Charlton Athletic, the Championship's 12th-placed club (6)

4 Wales midfielder, Robbie, relegated from the Premiership with Derby County (6)

8 Nickname of Lancashire's Spotland club that had its centenary year last season (4)

9 Leon, Everton midfield man who starred in the Toffees' UEFA Cup campaign (5)

10 Petr, Chelsea's European Champions League Final goalkeeper from Czech Republic (4)

13 - - - Dowie, manager appointed QPR boss in May 2008 (4)

14 Former Chelsea and Newcastle midfielder, Scott, with West Ham last season (6)

16 Sami, veteran Finland defender who has signed a new contract at Liverpool (6)

18 Aston Villa manager, Martin (6)

20 Glasgow giants who battled Rangers for the Scottish title (6)

22 Portsmouth's FA Cup Final centre back, Sylvain (6)

26 Wigan's former Liverpool and England striker, Emile (6)

28 England striker, Michael, appointed Newcastle skipper by manager Kevin Keegan (4)

31 Former Sheffield United boss now in London, - - - Warnock (4)

32 Bird that is the symbol of Championship play-off club, Crystal Palace (5)

33 Cameroon striker, Samuel, in Barcelona's Euro side beaten by Manchester United (4)

34 Nicky, Reading left back who made his England debut in summer 2007 (6)

35 - - - Pearce, former Manchester City boss in charge of England's successful Under-21 squad (6)

CLUES DOWN

2 Former Bolton boss, Sam, who lost his Newcastle United job last season (9)

3 Anfield's Israel international, - - - Benayoun (5)

4 - - - Given, keeper for Newcastle and Ireland (4)

5 Nationality of ex-Bolton wide man, Stelios Giannakopoulos (5)

6 Old Trafford's title-winning goalie, - - - van der Sar (5)

7 League position in which Arsenal finished the 2007-08 Premiership campaign (5)

11 Portsmouth's Senegal star, Papa Bouba (4)

12 Tottenham's young former Saints left-sided player, Gareth (4)

15 Club colour of Championship club Wolves (4)

17 Julio, Argentina midfielder who joined Middlesbrough from Sunderland (4)

19 Walkers Stadium club relegated from the Championship last term (9)

21 Young England striker - - - Walcott, breaking into Arsenal's first team (4)

23 Promising Cameroon defender, Alex, in Arsene Wenger's squad (4)

24 Country chosen to host the 2008 Olympic soccer tournament (5)

25 Chelsea's young Ivory Coast forward, Salomon (5)

27 Newcastle's former Man United and England star, Alan (5)

29 Country represented by 12 Down (5)

30 - - - Neville, Man United full back injured for almost the entire 2007-08 season (4)

EURO-ALL

There was no England team but we probably saw one of the best European Championships since 1996! Spain reigned supreme in Austria and Switzerland... and now we look at the other highlights of a magic tournament

SIZZLING SPAIN SNATCH SILVERWARE

With several Premiership-based players in the squad, the Spanish had added steel and strength, and finally tasted glory after 44 years without a major trophy.

A solid defence, held together by influential centre back Carles Puyol and expertly marshalled by keeper and captain Iker Casillas, formed the foundations.

The clever and creative element came from midfield, where Xavi, Andres Iniesta, David Silva and Cesc Fabregas ruled, and the goals were provided by the impressive strike duo of Fernando Torres and David Villa.

TURKISH FIGHT

It literally was the late, late, late show for Turkey as they scored crucial last-ditch goals against Switzerland, the Czech Republic and Croatia.

The fight back against the Czech Republic was spectacular, and the injury-time of extra-time equaliser against Croatia that came just three minutes after Slaven Bilic's men had taken the lead, was unbelievable.

The Turks impressive campaign was ended in the semi-final by Germany. Fatih Terim only had 13 outfield players available for the match but the Turks dominated for long periods and even took the lead, before going down 3-2 after Philipp Lahm grabbed a last-minute winner.

GREAT!

PREMIER LEAGUE-BASED TEAM OF THE TOURNAMENT FROM THE MOST IMPRESSIVE PLAYERS ON SHOW

1.	EDWIN VAN DER SAR	Holland	Man United
2.	JOSE BOSINGWA	Portugal	Chelsea
3.	VEDRAN CORLUKA	Croatia	Man City
4.	ANDRE OOIJER	Holland	Blackburn
5.	RICARDO CARVALHO	Portugal	Chelsea
6.	DECO	Portugal	Chelsea
7.	MICHAEL BALLACK	Germany	Chelsea
8.	CESC FABREGAS	Spain	Arsenal
9.	ROBIN VAN PERSIE	Holland	Arsenal
10.	FERNANDO TORRES	Spain	Liverpool
11.	LUKA MODRIC	Croatia	Tottenham

ENGLAND'S CONQUERORS IMPRESS

The teams that prevented England from competing in the tournament and signalled the end of Steve McClaren's reign as boss, Russia and Croatia, were in impressive form.

Both sides played entertaining football and reached the quarter-finals, with the Russians going one step further before being knocked out by Spain.

FIVE STARS

DAVID VILLA

The explosive striker fired Spain to glory, finishing as the tournament's top scorer with four goals. Villa scored a hat-trick against Russia and bagged a last-minute winner against Sweden in the group games. The Valencia man also notched a penalty against Italy in the quarter-final shoot-out, but missed the final after hobbling out of Spain's semi-final clash with Russia.

ANDREI ARSHAVIN

The technically brilliant attacking midfielder was the creative spark of Guus Hiddink's impressive Russia side. Arshavin missed his team's first two group games through suspension but returned to re-ignite their campaign with inspirational displays against Sweden and Holland. Not Andrei the giant in terms of size, but certainly in terms of stature.

XAVI

UEFA's Player of the Tournament and a major part of Spain's fluid and classy midfield, Xavi really made Luis Aragones' side tick. Quick-footed, technically gifted and with a great range of passing, the Barcelona man played the incisive through ball to create Fernando Torres' winner in the final and also bagged a goal of his own against Russia in the semi-final.

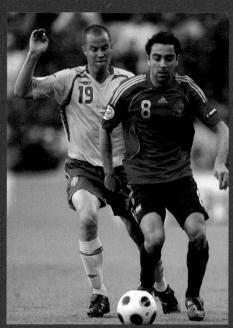

FIVE LET-DOWNS

CRISTIANO RONALDO

All the hype before the tournament was about one man… Cristiano Ronaldo. On the back of a spellbinding season with Manchester United, the tricky winger was expected to take the Euros by storm. But, possibly blighted by the daily transfer saga linking him to Real Madrid and a foot injury, he failed to find his best form. Cristiano grabbed one goal against the Czech Republic but failed to inspire Portugal past the quarter-finals.

PETR CECH

The usually reliable Chelsea stopper looked shaky at times and made a crucial mistake in the Czech Republic's decisive group game with Turkey. Cech fumbled a routine cross, allowing the Turks to level the scores at 2-2, before eventually winning the game 3-2. The result meant check mate for the Republic.

LUCA TONI

Italy's giant striker was expected to hit the goal trail following a prolific season in Germany with Bayern Munich. But Toni had a real shocker, and despite a whole host of opportunities he failed to score in any of the Azzurri's four matches.

MICHAEL BALLACK

Germany's inspirational captain played a major role in his country's march to the final. The Chelsea man scored twice, including a pile driver of a free-kick against Austria, and provided the guile and experience that the three-time European Champions desperately needed.

WESLEY SNEIJDER

Diminutive Dutch playmaker who brought imaginative passing and cutting edge to Marco van Basten's team. Sneijder scored two classy goals, a volley against Italy and a clever curling effort in the 4-1 demolition of France. The Real Madrid midfielder combined well with Rafael Van Der Vaart as Holland swept aside their Group C opponents, storming to the quarter-finals.

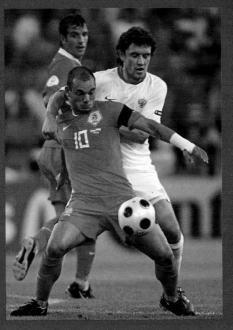

MICHAEL BALLACK

Blockbuster long-range free-kick against Austria which almost ripped the net.

ZLATAN IBRAHIMOVIC

Super Swede used his strength and skill to create a chance before slamming the ball into the top corner as the Scandinavians beat Greece.

NIHAT KAHVECI

The late winner for Turkey against Czech Republic. Nihat's neatly taken strike from the edge of the box that flew into the top corner was a real Turkish delight.

MARIO GOMEZ

Big things were expected of the young German striker who started the tournament up front alongside Miroslav Klose. After a couple of poor performances, which included a glaring missed open goal against Austria, the far-from-super Mario was dropped as Germany changed their tactics.

FRANCE

It was a case of "sacre bleu" for Les Bleus as the French failed to turn up at Euro 2008. Raymond Domenech's star-studded side drew 0-0 with Romania, were hammered 4-1 by Holland and were knocked out after a 2-0 defeat to Italy. Talents like Karim Benzema and Samir Nasri failed to shine and established stars such as Thierry Henry and Claude Makalele looked past their best.

IT'S A FAMILY AFFAIR

THEY SHARE SURNAMES BUT DON'T APPEAR VERY OFTEN IN THE SAME SIDES. MEET THE FOOTBALLING RELATIVES...

DAWSONS

There are three brothers in the Dawson family from Yorkshire, the most famous being **Michael**, the Spurs and England defender. He is the younger brother of Hull defender **Andy** and their middle brother **Kevin** played for Chesterfield. All three began their pro careers at Nottingham Forest.

SOARES

Battling ex-England Under-21 midfielder **Tom Soares** has made a name for himself at Crystal Palace. Elder brother **Louie**, who began his career with home-town club Reading, last year created his own piece of history.

Louie was part of the Aldershot side that returned to League football after a 16-year absence. The midfielder earned himself a new contract for his role in that success and became the Shots first-capped player when he turned out for Barbados.

WILKINS

Brighton boss **Dean Wilkins**, brother of former England and Man United star **Ray**, now a TV pundit, has kept the family's footballing traditions going for another few years. The Withdean gaffer signed his teenage son **Connor**.

ALONSOS

Midfield was the place dominated by **Xabi Alonso** at Liverpool at the same time as his brother **Mikel** was on loan at Bolton from Spanish side Real Sociedad – the club who sold Xabi to Anfield.

Back home in Spain their father, **Periko**, was a title-winner for Barcelona and other brother Jon is a referee.

LESCOTTS

England defender **Joleon Lescott** quickly established himself at Everton after his £5m move from Wolves and lifted the Toffees Player of the Season award in 2008.

Elder brother, **Aaron**, also a defender, plays for Bristol Rovers. He starred in wins against Southampton and Fulham in their run to the quarter-finals of the 2008 FA Cup.

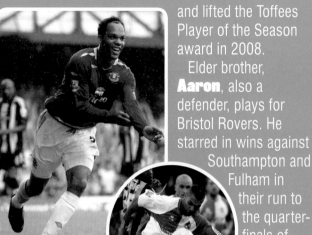

KANUS

Nwankwo Kanu made a name for himself at Arsenal before moving on to Wolves and then resurrected his career at Portsmouth under Harry Redknapp.

His trickery up front has led to some vital goals but the task of younger brother **Christopher** is to stop them going in at the other end.

Like his brother, the defender began his European career at Ajax. He also played for Alaves and Peterborough.

TERRYS

Chelsea defender **John Terry** and elder brother, **Paul**, a midfielder with Orient, have a bet each year on which of them will score the most goals. John has won hands down each season!

Their footballing family is extended by the fact that Paul is married to the sister of Fulham left-back **Paul Konchesky**.

KNOW YOUR FOOTBALL?

25 questions to check what you remember about season 2007-08!

WHO WAS THEIR CAPTAIN?

1. Arsenal   **3.** Liverpool   **5.** Bolton
2. Newcastle   **4.** Chelsea

MATCH THE SHIRTS AND NUMBERS

A. Man United 1   **C.** Arsenal 25   **E.** Everton 8
B. Newcastle 9   **D.** Liverpool 15

LAST SEASON...

1. Who were Premiership runners-up?
2. Which team were Championship champions?
3. Who was the Premier League's top scorer?
4. Which side just avoided relegation?
5. Who were bottom of the Championship?

WHICH COUNTRY?

1. Emmanuel Adebayor
2. Tim Cahill
3. Michael Essien
4. Habib Beye
5. Roque Santa Cruz

WINNERS

A. FA Cup   B. League Cup   C. Blue Square Premier   D. League One   E. SPL

GR-EIGHT!

EIGHT PREMIER LEAGUE STARS REVEAL WHAT THEY THINK ABOUT SOME OF THEIR OWN HEROES...

RIO FERDINAND
MAN UNITED

WAYNE ROONEY

"The thing about Wayne is that he keeps plugging away. He may miss a few chances but he keeps on getting in the right positions. If a forward isn't getting into the positions to score then you should be worried. But Wazza doesn't get too disheartened."

AARON HUGHES
FULHAM

DIMITAR BERBATOV

"His goal scoring record at international level is phenomenal and it is a difficult task marking him. He is as good as any striker around. People have been talking about a lot of money to buy him and they only do that when someone has a lot of ability."

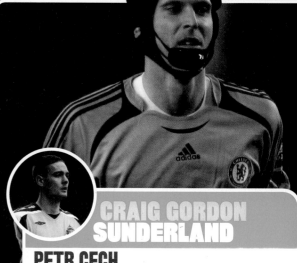

WAYNE ROONEY
MAN UNITED

PETER CROUCH

"Peter has been given quite a bit of stick at times, but he's played well, kept his head down and worked hard. He definitely gives England a different sort of option up front which is good to have. Defenders worry when he goes for crosses in the box."

CRAIG GORDON
SUNDERLAND

PETR CECH

"He has been here and done it for a few years now. Also Brad Friedel, Edwin van der Sar and David James. For guys like that to have done it at such a high level for such a long time is something you've got to look up to and admire."

JOHN TERRY
CHELSEA

SHAUN WRIGHT-PHILLIPS

"In terms of ability he's up there with Rooney. It's a relief to have him on our side rather than playing against him. He's a real threat, beats defenders and puts crosses in. He scores goals and makes goals."

EMMANUEL ADEBAYOR
ARSENAL

CRISTIANO RONALDO

"He is a good player with a lot of quality. Watching him play is something else, it is like watching a player on a PlayStation. He has so much quality and I have a lot of respect for what he has done."

CESC FABREGAS
ARSENAL

THEO WALCOTT

"Theo is so quick, so powerful. He is a very clever boy and he knows more than a player of his age should know. He is a great player and people expect a lot of him. I know from my experiences it takes time when you are young."

JAMIE CARRAGHER
LIVERPOOL

STEVEN GERRARD

"In the Champions League you play all the top teams and see some of the names they have got but Stevie's the one who does the decisive things in the end. He provides the big moment and that makes him one of the best players in the world."

FOOTIE OF THE FUTURE

FACT OR FANTASY? WE EXAMINE HOW FOOTBALL COULD DEVELOP IN THE NEXT FEW YEARS

LIVING AT THE GROUND

PREDICTION: You will be able to live in and around your favourite football grounds. Shops and everything else you need will create a special community.

FACT: Portsmouth are already planning this development.

MICROCHIP MANAGERS

PREDICTION: Managers will have technological and artificial intelligence aids to help make tactical decisions. But bosses and not computers will pick teams. Managers and referees will link directly to the teams as they play and players will have communicators.

FACT: Many top gaffers already use Pro Zone and other computer-generated information to keep a check on their players and make sure fitness is up to scratch.

MOBILE STADIUM

PREDICTION: Those unable to make the game will be able to watch on mobile phones, or upload matches to their PCs or games consoles. You may even get to join in the virtual action.

FACT: It's happening in various forms already, especially goal videos to mobile phones.

ROBO REFS

PREDICTION: Robotic linesmen and referees, spotlight systems and intelligent pitches will be used to eliminate human errors. Radio signals and laser pointers will determine where free-kicks and throw-ins should be taken.

FACT: Anything has to be better than some of the reffing we have seen recently! Would the laser zap a player who tries to steal too much distance for a throw or kick?

SPACE-AGE GRASS

PREDICTION: Grass pitches will be replaced by FieldTurf, a synthetic grass made from re-used car tyres. Water is drained away to be used elsewhere. Dry ice rockets could create heavy rainfall just before the game kicks-off.

FACT: This turf is already available. Some new stadia already have closing roofs and special sprinkler systems.

COOL KIT

PREDICTION: High-speed technology will be used to create boots to fit each player's feet. Keepers could wear protective suits to prevent injury! Sensors will be built into socks and shirts to keep a check on how players' bodies are performing during the game.
FACT: Players would still want lighter boots to make them run faster, bend shots better and carry the names of their kids!

INJURY IMMUNITY

PREDICTION: Injuries will be almost non-existent and medics may even predict them before they occur. Players will reach their peak by having their own specially formulated food and drinks. And if they do get injured new treatment methods will speed up recovery times.
FACT: Some new treatments are already being investigated – note how players now come back so fast from some injuries that would have kept them out months in the past.

INTERACTIVE GAMES

PREDICTION: New technology will allow miniature monitors at every seat where you can order food and drink for delivery. Vibrating seats will get you on your feet to sing! Scents could also get your excitement going!
FACT: Many reporters already have mini monitors – some toilets could do with different scents!

HOLOGRAPHIC VIEWING

PREDICTION: New 3D and computer-generated characters will make it feel like you are actually there when you watch on telly. Holographs will be used to fill empty seats of fans who leave before the end.
FACT: Mind-boggling tellys are released every few months. Would the holographs have to buy tickets?

SUPER SUPERSTARS!

PREDICTION: Our new footballers will be fitter than ever. They will cover almost twice the distance during games of our current stars – up to 20km! They will also be faster. But the bad news is they may have to train twice a day!
FACT: Agents will probably look for pay increases for more training.

● The predictions for the future were made in a special report for Orange, the phone and communications firm.

GIANT CROSSWORD

You can check out the answers on page 110 – but not until you have finished the questions.

CLUES ACROSS

1 Finland centre-back, - - - Hyypia, who completed nine years with Liverpool in 2008 (4)

3 Manchester City's young England defender, - - - Richards (5)

6 Korea star in Man United's title-winning side of 2008 (4)

8 Michael, defender who missed Tottenham's Carling Cup Final win through injury (6)

9 Spain midfield man, Mikel, who starred for UEFA Cup qualifiers Everton (6)

11 Patrice, French full-back of Champions, Manchester United (4)

13 Belarus man, Alexander, who completed his third season at Arsenal last term (4)

14 Jon Arne, full back whose own goal helped end Liverpool's Champions League run (5)

16 Derby's veteran former Everton centre-back, Alan (6)

17 Middlesbrough's England Under-21 midfielder, - - - Johnson (4)

18 Club emblem of Championship play-off winners Hull (5)

19 Man City full-back, Michael, who joined in January 2007 (4)

20 Aston Villa's 2007-08 club captain, - - - Barry (6)

22 - - - Mendez, Portsmouth and Portugal midfielder (5)

23 Colour sported by Chelsea in the 2008 Champions League Final (4)

24 Zoltan, Hungarian who helped West Brom to promotion (4)

27 Ghana's star midfield man, Michael, at Stamford Bridge (6)

29 Former Gunner, Patrick – winner of the Italian title with Inter (6)

30 Ki-hyeon, South Korea forward taken to Craven Cottage from Reading (4)

31 British nationals such as David Moyes and Sir Alex Ferguson (5)

32 Hangings draped around the goalposts (4)

CLUES DOWN

1 Reading and Nigeria centre-back, Sam, loaned to Charlton Athletic last season (5)

2 Emiliano, Argentine left-back who broke into the Liverpool side in May 2008 (5)

3 English city that staged the 2008 UEFA Cup Final (10)

4 Shirt colour sported by Burnley last season (6)

5 Middlesbrough's German-born former Chelsea defender, Robert (4)

6 - - - Nevin, former Scotland winger now working as a TV and radio pundit (3)

7 Roy, manager who kept Sunderland in the Premiership in 2008 (5)

10 Former Arsenal and France Under-21 forward, Jeremie, who joined Middlesbrough in 2007 (9)

12 Wayne, former Spurs and Palace winger who joined Villa for £1.25m in January (9)

15 Manchester United and England midfield star, Owen (10)

21 Xabi, Spain midfielder who completed three years at Anfield in 2008 (6)

22 Welshman, Tony – the manager who led Stoke City into the Premiership (5)

24 West Ham and England keeper, Robert (5)

25 Tony, former Arsenal skipper – assistant manager of FA Cup winners, Portsmouth (5)

26 Edinburgh Scottish Premier League club now managed by Mixu Paatelainen (4)

28 England defender recalled last season after great Premiership form, - - - Campbell (3)

2

7

24

28

WHOSE BOOTS?

WE REVEAL THE FOOTWEAR FAVOURED BY SOME OF THE PREMIERSHIP'S STAR PLAYERS – WHETHER THEY ARE TOUGH DEFENDERS, CREATIVE MIDFIELDERS OR HOT-SHOT STRIKERS

DAVID BENTLEY

Puma boots are the preferred choice for the nippy and skilled England winger as he pumps over crosses from the right.

WAYNE ROONEY

Nike Mercurial boots are slipped on to the England and Manchester United striker's feet when he gets ready to torment defences.

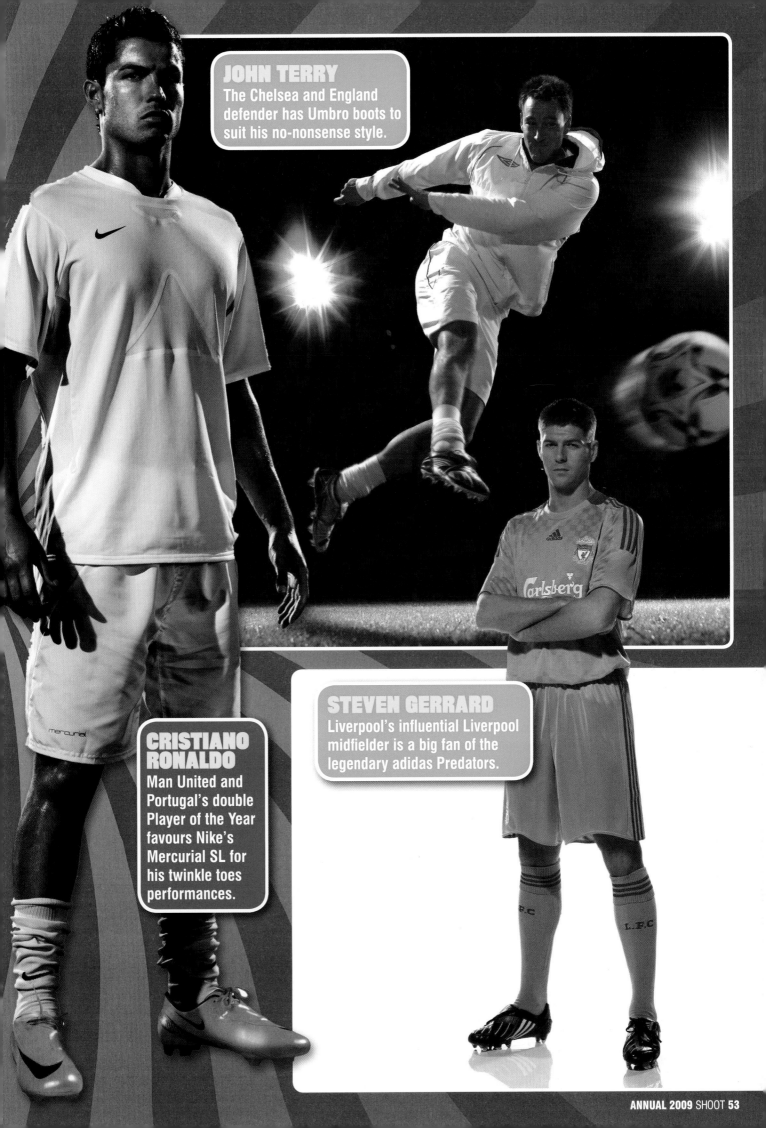

JOHN TERRY
The Chelsea and England defender has Umbro boots to suit his no-nonsense style.

CRISTIANO RONALDO
Man United and Portugal's double Player of the Year favours Nike's Mercurial SL for his twinkle toes performances.

STEVEN GERRARD
Liverpool's influential Liverpool midfielder is a big fan of the legendary adidas Predators.

10 THINGS YOU NEED TO KNOW ABOUT CRISTIANO RONALDO

1 Ronaldo – full name Cristiano Ronaldo dos Santos Aveiro – was born in Funchal, the capital of Madeira, on February 5, 1985.

2 Ronaldo joined Manchester United in 2003. The story goes that the players persuaded Sir Alex Ferguson to sign the then 18-year-old Sporting Lisbon winger on the plane home after they played a pre-season friendly against the club. Fergie had already watched him play.

3 In United's comprehensive 6-0 win over Newcastle United last season, Ronaldo secured not only his 50th league goal for the Reds but also his first-ever hat-trick for the team.

4 Cristiano's Dad, Dinis, named him after his favourite actor – former USA president Ronald Reagan.

5 Winger Ronaldo was the highest goalscorer in the Premier League in 2007-2008 with 31. His closest rivals were Emmanuel Adebayor of Arsenal and Fernando Torres of Liverpool with 24 strikes each.

6 Ronaldo has some fans in high places – here's what experts said about the superstar. "In my opinion he is the best player in the world" – Blackburn keeper Brad Friedel. "Cristiano Ronaldo right now is a 10 out of 10, the best in the world" – Real Madrid manager Bernd Schuster. "Ronaldo is better than George Best and Denis Law, who were two brilliant and great players in the history of United" – Holland legend Johan Cruyff.

7 Ronaldo won the Professional Footballers' Association Player of the Year award for the second year in a row in 2008, beating such stars as Fernando Torres, Steven Gerrard, Cesc Fabregas and Emmanuel Adebayor. He also picked up the Football Writers' Association footballer of the year title, again for a second year.

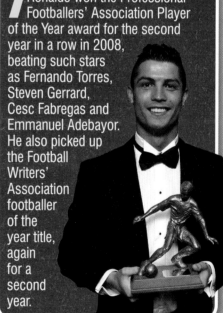

8 Ronaldo's nickname as a younger player was "Abelhinha" which translates as "Little Bee"!

9 Ronaldo scored eight goals during Portugal's Euro 2008 qualifying campaign, taking his international tally to 20 at the time.

10 Ronaldo scored two goals or more in NINE Premier League games last season. The highlight came during Man United's 6-0 victory over Newcastle at Old Trafford when he hit a hat-trick.

CRISTIANO
RONALDO

DAYS OFF

FOOTBALLERS USED TO GO DOWN THE PUB AND BETTING SHOP WHEN THEY FINISHED TRAINING… BUT NO LONGER!

DEFENSIVE ROCK
CHRISTIAN DAILLY

Scotland defender Christian Dailly is lead singer and guitarist in powerpop-indie rock ban South Playground, formed with three friends.

The former West Ham star, who starred for Rangers last term, has even heard his most famous song, *Scale Free*, played over the loudspeakers at Hampden Park.

WILD ROVERS
MORTEN GAMST PEDERSEN

Morten Gamst Pedersen is more famous in his home country of Norway than his king – thanks to being a member of a boy band!

With four other footballers he formed The Players who had a No.1 hit in their homeland with *This Is For Real*. They donated their profits to a charity called Soccer Against Crime.

Fellow Blackburn striker Roque Santa Cruz scored a Top 40 hit in Austria and Germany when he sang with rock band Sportfreunde Stiller.

A DIFFERENT BALL GAME...
ROBIN VAN PERSIE

Robin van Persie's a bit of a star when it comes to playing with a ball far smaller than the one he is more usually associated with.

The Arsenal and Holland striker is red-hot at running down wings with a full-sized football but is also a smash hit at table tennis.

He is so good that he got an invite to take part in a celebrity event at the Dunlop Masters staged in London's swish Albert Hall.

STOPPER TAKES AIM
STEVE HARPER

Long-serving Newcastle keeper Steve Harper is a bit of a sports fanatic when he gets a chance.

He likes to take in a round of golf with fellow shot-stopper Shay Given, is qualified to referee lower league football games and is a bit useful with a cricket bat!

But watch out when he takes aim on a darts board! He's a hot-shot with the arrows and even gave darts ace Phil "The Power" Taylor a run for his money in an exhibition game.

MC CLINT!
CLINT DEMPSEY

Fulham and USA midfielder Clint Dempsey is really rapper "Deuce" and has a video on YouTube called *Don't Tread*, featuring Big Hawk and XO. Key words: clint dempsey deuce don't tread

RACING CERTAINTY
MICHAEL OWEN

Newcastle United and England striker Michael Owen is horseracing mad!

Not only is he big mates with champion jockey Frankie Dettori but the former Liverpool and Real Madrid forward even has his own stables.

Michael aims to breed and train horses when he hangs up his boots and along with members of his family can often be seen enjoying a day out at the races.

When one of his horses stormed past the finishing line first, Michael dashed out of a Newcastle betting shop and started to celebrate.

"When she won I couldn't help myself, I just opened the door of the bookies and ran up and down the street," admitted Michael.

LOVELY GRUB

Forget about caviar and prawn sarnies – our Premier League heroes love the same snacks as us fans...

NUTS FOR DOUGH

ARSENAL stars drive manager Arsene Wenger nuts – or to be more precise doughnuts!

They just love wicked doughnuts from Krispy Kreme shops after playing a game and on their days off.

The French gaffer hasn't yet cracked down on his stars munching on their favourite fattening food, which is more than can be said for his North London rival Juande Ramos.

The Tottenham chief outlawed biscuits, cakes and sweets when he arrived at White Hart Lane and saw the pounds drop off some of his overweight stars.

SPANISH OMELETTE

The Spanish players on Merseyside knock down the Liverpool-Everton barriers to cook up regular banquets. Everton's Mikel Arteta shares meals and football talk when he visits the homes of Liverpool rivals Pepe Reina, Xabi Alonso and Fernando Torres.

"They also come to mine and we all get on perfectly well and respect the fact we play for rival clubs," said Arteta.

NO PLACE LIKE HOME

Home cooking wins hands down for Portugal winger Cristiano Ronaldo.

"I can eat English food but mostly we eat Portuguese food at home," he admits. "Any of my family who are staying with me will do the cooking."

PIZZA ACTION

DEAN ASHTON can be hot stuff playing up front – no surprise when you learn that his favourite food is a Domino's pepperoni pizza!

The West Ham and England striker reckons if he could only live on one food it would be his favourite pizza delivery.

BREAST MEAL

MIKEL ARTETA wasn't impressed by the fish and chips he found on offer at Everton's club restaurant so he got the chefs to cook up his favourite dishes!

He took in his own rice, tomato sauce, garlic and onions and got them preparing his favourite pasta and chicken breast too!

MUNCH BOX...

"After games I have fish and chips, Indian and Chinese. Yeah, altogether! It's the one time I can eat junk food and I need the protein. If I eat pasta I am starving within an hour."
Reading and USA keeper Marcus Hahnemann gets an attack of the munchies!

"Spaghetti Bolognese with plenty of mushrooms. My missus makes it. That's a superstition as well because I have spag bol on a Friday night if we're playing at home…"
England star David Bentley is a pasta master….

"Spaghetti carbonara. A healthy diet is key to a healthy mind and body."
England striker Peter Crouch also confesses to a love of spinach. Wonder if that's what made him so tall!

LET US TAKE YOU AROUND
THE CLUBS

ROBIN VAN PERSIE

POSITION: Striker
BORN: August 6, 1983, Rotterdam
PREVIOUS CLUBS: Feyenoord
FACT: Despite a whole series of injuries that have limited his appearances the Dutchman, boss Arsene Wenger rates £3m van Persie as a "world-class" player.

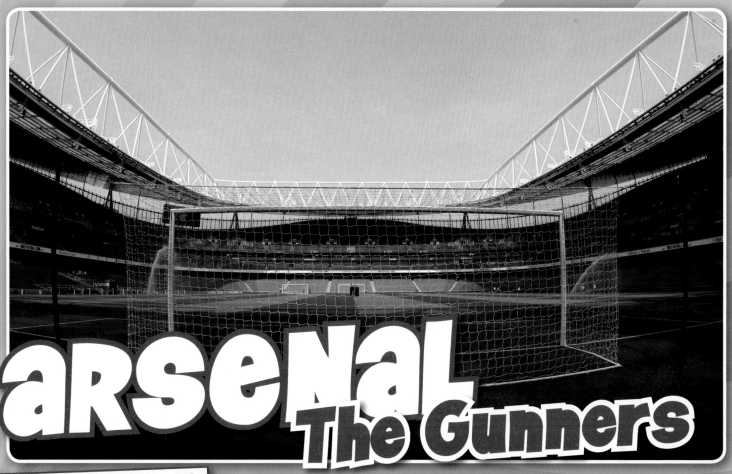

ARSENAL
The Gunners

SEASON 2007-08

PREMIER LEAGUE: 3rd
FA CUP: Round 5, Man United 5 Arsenal 0
LEAGUE CUP: Semi-final, Spurs 6 Arsenal 2 (two legs)
EUROPE: Champions League, quarter-final, Arsenal 3 Liverpool 5 (two legs)
HIGH POINT: Winning 3-2 at Bolton after their ten men were trailing 2-0
LOW POINT: Losing 5-1 at arch-rivals Tottenham in the second leg of the semi-final of the Carling Cup, their first defeat in 21 derby clashes under Wenger.

PLAYER OF THE SEASON

CESC FABREGAS, the PFA Young Player of the Year, showed creativity and vision to help Arsenal dominate games in what was always going to be a difficult year. He finished the campaign with 13 goals and Real Madrid still insisting they wanted to prise the star away from London despite his long term contract at The Emirates. His blistering form at the European Championships will have raised his value even further.

STAR PLAYER EMMANUEL ADEBAYOR

POSITION: Striker **BORN:** February 26, 1984, Lome, Togo **TRANSFER VALUE:** £18m

BEING CALLED THE "NEW THIERRY HENRY"
"When the boss says that I am happy but the most important thing is to prove he is not wrong. I am doing my best and it is going well."

IMPROVED FORM
"When Thierry left, guys like me and Robin van Persie knew we were going to play so we concentrated even more. Thierry would score 30 goals a season, now we don't have anyone who we can be sure will hit that target so we put our heart into the game."

GOAL TARGETS
"I could say I want to score 30 but if I got to that total by March what would I do? Am I going to stop then? I never set a target – it is just important to keep scoring and winning."

PLAYING FOR ARSENAL
"The team is full of talented players but if you don't put a bit of heart inside each other it can be difficult. We have talented players and good team mates and we love each other. We believe in ourselves and the boss."

BOSS ARSENE WENGER SAYS...
"Adebayor has made one of the biggest improvements in his finishing of any player I have seen. What I liked when I bought him was that he can give you the option in the air yet he doesn't immobilise your game."

IT'S A FACT!
- He's nearly as fast as Thierry Henry... but faster over 100m than Theo Walcott!
- He can jump as high as a basketball player.
- He scores more than a quarter of his goals with headers.
- His passing rate is one of the best in the Premier League for a striker.

ASTON VILLA
The Villans

SEASON 2007-08

PREMIER LEAGUE: 6th
FA CUP: Third round, Villa 0 Man United 2
LEAGUE CUP: Third round, Villa 0 Leicester City 1
EUROPE: n/a
HIGH POINT: Crushing Birmingham 5-1 in the Second City derby game.
LOW POINT: Missing out on a place in Europe on the final day of the season, although they did get an Inter Toto place!

PLAYER OF THE SEASON

GARETH BARRY was the eighth best player in the Premier League last term according to the official Opta stats. He was one of the league's top passers and easily Villa's best distributor of the ball. He also added eight goals and earned himself an England recall along the way.

STAR PLAYER GABBY AGBONLAHOR

POSITION: Striker **BORN:** October 13, 1986, Birmingham **TRANSFER VALUE:** £5m

LEARNING THE GAME
"I like the way Martin O'Neill manages. He talks to all of us individually, and also as a group. He told me I'm good enough to be playing at this level and that has given me the confidence to go out on the pitch and hopefully play my best."

COMPETITION FOR PLACES
"It's great having good players at the club. I can learn a lot from them, but I also want to compete with them. I want them to have to be playing well to keep me out of the team."

HIS FIRST START
"To score on my debut against Everton was different class although losing 4-1 was not the result we wanted! When the gaffer said I was playing, I thought: 'Grab the chance.'"

HIS STRENGTHS
"I like to run at defenders and use my pace, my main asset. When I get the ball I always look to go past the first man. The gaffer tells me that if there's

a telling pass on I have to consider that first."

BIGGEST INFLUENCE
"Dad says he knows a lot about football and tells me what I should be doing, but I'm not so sure how good he was."

BOSS MARTIN O'NEILL SAYS
"What Gabby has done for us has been fantastic. Some strikers live by goals, but there are exceptions to the rule. His contribution at times is fantastic."

IT'S A FACT!

• David O'Leary gave Gabby his debut but O'Neill has turned him into a regular first teamer.
• He could have played for Nigeria (father), Scotland (mother) but chose England.

• Gabby was offered a place in Villa's academy at the age of 14.
• He scored 40 goals a season for the club's youth side.
• He had games on loan at Watford and Sheffield Wednesday.

POSITION: Striker
BORN: September 5, 1979, Lorenskog, Norway
PREVIOUS CLUBS: Valerenga, Rosenborg, Valencia, AS Roma (loan), Besiktas, Lyon
FACT: John was Norway's first black player when he made his international debut in November 1998.

JOHN CAREW

ROQUE SANTA CRUZ

POSITION: Striker
BORN: August 16, 1981, Ascuncion, Paraguay
PREVIOUS CLUBS: Olimpia Asuncion, Bayern Munich
FACT: The former Paraguay Footballer of the Year has twice won the league title in his home country but he failed to make a big impression during his time in Germany.

BLACKBURN Rovers

SEASON 2007-08

PREMIER LEAGUE: 7th
FA CUP: Third round, Blackburn 1 Coventry 4
LEAGUE CUP: Quarter-final,
Blackburn 2 Arsenal 3 (aet)
EUROPE: UEFA Cup first round,
Rovers 2 Larissa 3 (two legs)
HIGH POINT: The form of David Bentley,
Chris Samba and Roque Santa Cruz.
LOW POINT: Failure at the first hurdle in both
the UEFA and FA Cups to lesser opposition.

PLAYER OF THE SEASON

ROCQUE SANTA CRUZ was the Fans' Player
of the Year. He agreed a four-year deal when
he signed in summer 2007 from Bayern
Munich. The German giants don't normally let
good players go but the £3.5m they sold the
6ft 2in striker for now appears a bargain after
his 23 goals from his first season in England.

STAR PLAYER DAVID BENTLEY

POSITION: Striker **BORN:** August 27, 1984,
Peterborough **TRANSFER VALUE:** £12m

LEAVING ARSENAL
"I needed regular football. It's hard to break
into a great team like Arsenal – you have to
be exceptional in a series of games rather
than just one to keep your place."

PLAYING FOOTBALL
"I have a nice car and a nice house, but football
has to be about fun, about enjoyment. Honestly,
I don't care how much I'm paid, if I wasn't
enjoying it, I'd pack it in."

FORMER BOSS MARK HUGHES
"He won't try to be your friend, having a laugh
and a joke. He doesn't want to sit down for
coffee. He and Mr Capello are my favourite
kind of manager: disciplined."

FABIO CAPELLO
"With him we could win the
World Cup. If it was solely down to
individual talent, we would already
be the best team in the world, we just
need to learn to play together."

FAVOURITE PLAYER
"Kaka. I'd stick him in the middle of the park
and let him pull all the strings. He's still
young, but he's a top player and I think he's
going to have a really good career. I think
he'd do well in England."

BOSS PAUL INCE SAYS
"We are obviously going to have to
deal with a lot of speculation about
David. But as far as I'm concerned,
I want him here."

IT'S A FACT!

• Arsene Wenger admits he made
a mistake by selling Bentley.
• He was booed by England fans
after pulling out of an Under-21
tournament because he was tired.
• David hopes to take the number

seven England shirt worn by the
man he could be destined to
replace, David Beckham.
• He uses the same agent
Thierry Henry had when
he played at Arsenal.

BOLTON The Trotters

SEASON 2007-08

PREMIER LEAGUE: 16th
FA CUP: Third round, Bolton 0 Sheffield United 1
LEAGUE CUP: Fourth round, Bolton 0 Man City 1
EUROPE: UEFA Cup last 16, Bolton 1 Sporting Lisbon 2 (two legs)
HIGH POINT: Drawing in Germany against Bundesliga leaders Bayern Munich in the UEFA Cup.
LOW POINT: Losing the local derby against Blackburn Rovers 4-1.

PLAYER OF THE SEASON

Although not officially the Player of the Season, **GARY CAHILL** was without doubt a shining star during his first year at The Reebok and did earn an award as the fans' brightest new talent. The defender signed from Aston Villa during the January 2008 transfer window for a fee that could reach £5m.

STAR PLAYER KEVIN DAVIES

POSITION: Striker **BORN:** March 26, 1977, Sheffield **TRANSFER VALUE:** £1m

BEST FOOTBALL MOMENT
"I would have to say reaching the Carling Cup Final with Bolton in 2004. We lost to Middlesbrough but being there was special."

BEST PLAYER FACED
"I always have a good battle against John Terry. I've caught him a couple of times and given him a bloody lip, and he's caught me, but that's the way it should be… just get up and get on with the game."

FAVOURITE PLAYER
"Wayne Rooney. He's an intelligent player, he's got age on his side, can play in a number of positions and he thinks a lot faster than most."

BOSS GARY MEGSON
"He came in and picked up a bunch of lads who were really down at the time. Confidence was probably at rock-bottom and we were rock-bottom of the table. He lifted the place and training became fun again."

BOSS GARY MEGSON SAYS
"He gives some fantastic performances. When everything clicks he's as good as anything in the country even though some people tend to think he does not get as many goals as he should."

IT'S A FACT!

• Members of Bolton's junior club last season voted Kev the player their mums most-fancied!
• Southampton sold the striker to Blackburn for £7.5m, got him back for Egil Ostenstad and £1.2m and then let him move to Bolton on a free in 2003.
• The hitman is sponsored by a Lord and two local MPs!
• He has played three times for England Under-21s.

KEVIN NOLAN

POSITION: Midfielder
BORN: June 24, 1982, Liverpool
PREVIOUS CLUBS: None
FACT: Captain Kevin was the first product of the club's Premiership academy having signed for them at the age of 14.

POSITION: Midfielder
BORN: November 8, 1981,
Romford, Essex
PREVIOUS CLUBS: West Ham
FACT: Joe joined Chelsea in 2003
for £6.6m and refused to be shipped out on loan
to CSKA Moscow by former boss Claudio Ranieri.

JOE COLE

CHELSEA
The Blues

SEASON 2007-08

PREMIER LEAGUE: 2nd
FA CUP: Quarter-final, Barnsley 1 Chelsea 0
LEAGUE CUP: Final, Chelsea 1 Spurs 2
EUROPE: Champions League Final, Man United 1 v Chelsea 1 (aet, Chelsea lost 6-5 on penalties
HIGH POINT: Beating Man United with four games to go to open up the title race.
LOW POINT: Losing the European Cup Final.

PLAYER OF THE SEASON

JOE COLE had arguably his best season in blue, picking up the supporters' Player of the Year award. He's jinked his way around defenders, made decisive passes and proved to many that he has the ability to last the distance and influence games.

STAR PLAYER: JOHN TERRY

POSITION: Defender **BORN:** December 7, 1980, Dagenham, East London **TRANSFER VALUE:** £25m

PREM OR EUROPE?
"I think the Premiership has got to be our base every year if we want to go on and dominate football in all competitions. That's our aim. I'd love to be lifting that trophy again next May."

PREPARATION
"I've got my own little things I do during the week as I approach a game. I've got my normal routine when I'm in the dressing room and yes, I have superstitions. But I'm not telling you what they are!"

THE FUTURE
"I'd like to manage one day. When I was speaking about my contract with Chelsea, we spoke about an option to manage at the end of it. I want to get my badges and then make the decision."

FAVOURITE PLAYER
"Wayne Rooney is a fantastic footballer. During my first training session with

him for England he came on the pitch and beat four or five players and flicked the ball over the keeper!"

IT'S A FACT!

- JT joined Chelsea at the age of 14 and started as a midfielder.
- He was picked as England's captain under Steve McClaren.
- A loan spell of just six games

at Nottingham Forest kick-started his career.
- His elder brother Paul is a midfielder with Leyton Orient but has also played for Yeovil.

everTON
The Toffees

SEASON 2007-08

PREMIER LEAGUE: 5th
FA CUP: Third round, Everton 0 Oldham 1
LEAGUE CUP: Semi-final,
Chelsea 3 Everton 1 (two legs)
EUROPE: UEFA Cup last 16,
Everton 2 Fiorentina 2 (two legs, Everton
lost 4-2 on pens aet)
HIGH POINT: Ensuring a place in the UEFA
Cup with a final day victory over Newcastle.
LOW POINT: Crashing out of the FA Cup at
the first hurdle to League One side Oldham.

PLAYER OF THE SEASON

JOLEON LESCOTT will cost Everton a total
of £5m but after his first Premier League
season it looks like money well spent. The
former Wolves defender can play central
defence or at left-back and also has a knack
of raiding forward to score and set up goals.
Has also pushed his case for England.

STAR PLAYER TIM CAHILL

POSITION: Midfielder **BORN:** December 6, 1979,
Sydney, Australia. **TRANSFER VALUE:** £7m

LOOK AND LEARN
"I want to be a massive part of it when I am
injured, just like when I am playing. It's difficult
to watch, but it's very educational as you see
things from a different perspective. I have
learned a lot from watching and have been
able to pass information to the lads."

COMPETITION FOR PLACES
"I think every team needs more players.
The healthiest thing about football is if you
bring in other players it makes the others
better by creating more competition. I will
always welcome newcomers to give a new
spark or take the limelight away from some
of the bigger players."

FIRST PREMIERSHIP GOAL
"I remember running off and pulling my shirt
over my head against Man City and running
straight into a red card! It's a moment
which will be remembered forever."

THE PREMIERSHIP
"There are so many people watching
you and they see everything – your
mistakes and the things that you do
well. You're analysed so much. It's
certainly quicker and more physical
than playing in The Championship."

BOSS DAVID MOYES SAYS
"He is so important to us. I don't send
him out telling him to score goals.
He always goes out to score."

IT'S A FACT!

• Cahill was the first player
ever to score for Australia in
the finals of a World Cup.
• He cost Everton a bargain
£2m from Millwall in 2004.
• Tim showed respect and refused
to celebrate when he scored
for Everton against Millwall
in the FA Cup.
• Tim played once for the
Under-20s Western Samoa
team – at the age of 14!

AYEGBENI YAKUBU

POSITION: Striker
BORN: November 22, 1982, Benin, Nigeria
PREVIOUS CLUBS: Maccabi Haifa, Hapoel Kfar Saba (loan), Portsmouth, Middlesbrough
FACT: Everton paid a club record £11.25m to Middlesbrough to sign the Nigeria striker in August 2007.

Everton

SIMON DAVIES

POSITION: Midfielder
BORN: October 23, 1979, Haverfordwest, Wales
PREVIOUS CLUBS: Peterborough, Tottenham, Everton
FACT: Simon has won more than 50 caps for Wales and scored in a shock 2-1 victory against Italy.

FULHAM
The Cottagers

SEASON 2007-08

PREMIER LEAGUE: 17th
FA CUP: Third round, Bristol Rovers 0
Fulham 0 (replay after 2-2, Fulham lost
penalty shoot out 5-2 aet)
LEAGUE CUP: Third round,
Fulham 1 Bolton 2 (aet)
EUROPE: n/a
HIGH POINT: Winning 1-0 at Pompey on the
final day to guarantee Premier League safety.
LOW POINT: Being without the influential
Jimmy Bullard for all but the last 17 games.

PLAYER OF THE SEASON

SIMON DAVIES started all but one of the
Cottagers' league games last season, his
first full campaign since arriving in January
2007 from Everton. The Wales midfielder only
grabbed a handful of goals – which included
a spectacular free-kick against Sunderland
– but his all round contribution and work rate
made him a firm fans' favourite.

STAR PLAYER: JIMMY BULLARD

POSITION: Midfielder **BORN:** October 23, 1978,
Newham, East London **TRANSFER VALUE:** £4m

PLAYING IN THE PREMIER LEAGUE
"I always believed I could play in the Premier
League but it happened so quickly after I signed
for Wigan. I'd only been there three years and
when I joined we were in League One."

FAVOURITE GROUNDS
"I always wanted to play at Anfield. You come
out to the song *You'll Never Walk Alone* and
that was class. I've played at West Ham a few
times, where I was as a kid, and that is another
massive game for me."

KEEPING ON PLAYING
"I had a bad dead leg against
Middlesbrough but I didn't want to come
off. I went out at half-time trying to warm
it up. I should have come off but I just love
to be playing."

MISSING A SEASON INJURED
"It was hard, horrible. I went to every game
to watch my team which was the hardest part. I
couldn't even think about playing but I came
back stronger and fitter."

ALL-ACTION
"I give 100 per cent every day,
even in training. On match days
I'll go 100 or 110 per cent."

BOSS ROY HODGSON SAYS....
"Jimmy loves to be in that attacking midfield
role. I think we can get more out of him in the
offensive side of the game. I think he's got
goals in him and he can also set them up."

IT'S A FACT!

• Jimmy is a pretty useful golfer
who could even turn pro.
• He was on the books at West
Ham at the same time as Joe
Cole and Frank Lampard.

• Bully is a top match angler
who fishes for Dorking, the Real
Madrid of the fishing world!
• He set a new record at Wigan,
playing 120 consecutive games.

HULL CITY
The Tigers

SEASON 2007-08

CHAMPIONSHIP: Play-off winners
FA CUP: Fourth round, Plymouth 3 Hull 2
LEAGUE CUP: Third round, Hull 0 Chelsea 4
EUROPE: n/a
HIGH POINT: The Wembley winner by Dean Windass in the play-off final!
LOW POINT: Losing 3-0 at Preston then 4-0 at Southampton within four black days during December.

PLAYER OF THE SEASON

Defender **MICHAEL TURNER'S** three Player of the Year awards, including Players' Player, is testament to his contribution to the promotion campaign. The former Brentford man was also the Supporters' Player of the Year the previous campaign, his first with the Tigers.

STAR PLAYER: DEAN WINDASS

POSITION: Striker **BORN:** April 1, 1969, Hull **TRANSFER VALUE:** £250k

PREMIERSHIP PROMOTION
"If someone had said we'd be one game away from the Premier League at the end of the season I'd have laughed in their face. Running out at Wembley for my home-town club with my wife and kids there and millions watching was the proudest day of my life."

HIS WEMBLEY WINNER
'It was unbelievable. It's absolutely surreal to score the winning goal. Fraizer Campbell picked me out and I just volleyed it and couldn't believe it when it went into the top corner."

BOSS PHIL BROWN
"I'm old enough to have played against the gaffer and he was a very good right-back who passed the ball properly. Passing was Phil's method of playing and now, as a manager, he's gone back to it."

LEGENDS
"People use that word too much in football and I don't like it. I'm not a legend,

I'm a footballer. I don't like that phrase because you get people like those that go and fight for the country in Iraq and those sorts of places, and I get paid a lot of money to just kick a football about and do something I enjoy."

BOSS PHIL BROWN SAYS
"Not many carry on playing at his age, but he's that special breed, like Teddy Sheringham. He can play into his 40s. He looks after himself, retains his fitness and his enthusiasm."

IT'S A FACT!

• Deano worked on local building sites when he was first rejected by Hull as a youngster.
• His winning goal in the play-off final at Wembley is expected to earn City around £60m.
• Windass was 30 before he played in the Premiership, with Bradford City in 1999. He also played in the top flight with Boro.

POSITION: Striker
BORN: October 26, 1982, Leeds
PREVIOUS CLUBS: Leeds United, Rushden and Diamonds, Chesterfield, Wigan
FACT: Folan, who had one game on loan at Hull in 2001, was their record buy when he joined them for £1m on transfer deadline day, August 2007.

CALEB FOLAN

POSITION: Striker
BORN: March 20, 1984, Madrid, Spain
PREVIOUS CLUBS: Atletico Madrid
FACT: Nando's grandfather was a massive Atletico fan and used to take him to games. He was also the first person the young striker called after making his debut and scoring for the Spanish club's youth side.

FERNANDO TORRES

LIVERPOOL The Reds

SEASON 2007-08

PREMIER LEAGUE: 4th
FA CUP: Fifth round, Liverpool 1 Barnsley 2
LEAGUE CUP: Quarter-final, Chelsea 2 Liverpool 0
EUROPE: Champions League semi-final, Liverpool 3 Chelsea 4 (two legs)
HIGH POINT: The blistering form of Torres, and his hat-tricks against Reading, West Ham and Middlesbrough.
LOW POINT: Crashing out of the FA Cup to Championship strugglers Barnsley thanks to a 93rd-minute goal from Brian Howard.

PLAYER OF THE SEASON

How many supporters would have expected **FERNANDO TORRES** to settle in so quickly after his club record £25m move from Atletico Madrid? We all knew he was a skilled and tricky player with a knack of scoring but to smack home 24 Premiership goals in your debut season is some going. And to be talked about in the same breath as Ian Rush and Kenny Dalglish makes him pretty special!

STAR PLAYER STEVEN GERRARD

POSITION: Midfielder **BORN:** May 30, 1980, Liverpool **TRANSFER VALUE:** £30m

EURO STARS
"It's not down to me to say who is and who isn't a good side but we are and you can't argue with our record. We don't fear anyone in Europe and when other teams see our record they can't look forward to playing us."

CONSISTENCY
"You can play well for most of the year but if you fail in the last few games you can end up with nothing – but that's football."

TORRES
"He's been fantastic for us. He is one of the best players I have ever played with or against. I compared him to Ian Rush a while ago and I wouldn't come out with something like that lightly. We play as a team but we have a match-winner in Fernando."

BEING SKIPPER
"As captain I have a lot of responsibility and I thrive on big games. If you can't be up for the big matches you probably shouldn't be playing."

BOSS RAFA BENITEZ SAYS
"With the freedom he has now and his quality going forward, he's unstoppable. The understanding with Torres is also very good. It could be that they bring out the best in each other. He knows what we expect from him and he plays well in virtually every game."

IT'S A FACT!

- He became Liverpool captain in 2003-04, the same season that also saw him skipper England.
- Former Liverpool favourite Kevin Keegan gave Gerrard his England debut against Ukraine in 2000.
- He was spotted by Liverpool when he was just nine-years-old and signed as a professional for the club when he became 17.
- The Queen awarded an MBE to Stevie G in 2007.

MANCHESTER CITY
The Citizens

SEASON 2007-08

PREMIER LEAGUE: 9th
FA CUP: Fourth round,
Sheffield United 2 Man City 1
LEAGUE CUP: Quarter-final,
Man City 0 Spurs 2
EUROPE: n/a
HIGH POINT: Doing the double over bitter
Manchester rivals United.
LOW POINT: Failing to qualify for Europe
after a blistering start to the season.

PLAYER OF THE SEASON

The future of defender RICHARD DUNNE
was in doubt following the departure of boss
Sven Goran Eriksson. But new manager Mark
Hughes made his first priority a new contract
for the Republic of Ireland star, who was
Player of the Year for a fourth successive
season. He appears to have been around
forever but Dunny is still only 29.

STAR PLAYER: MARTIN PETROV

POSITION: Midfielder **BORN:** January 15, 1979,
Vratsa, Bulgaria **TRANSFER VALUE:** £6m

SENT OFF FOR BULGARIA
"I just couldn't stop crying. I was sobbing on
the sidelines. I didn't play for my country for
a year after a previous red card for the
Under-18s and my first game back happened
to be my senior debut."

PREMIERSHIP TEAM MATES
"When you are playing with good footballers
around you it is much easier to gel. Nearly all
of them play for their national teams so they
have great experience. The players here
know what to do."

LANGUAGES
"I can speak German, French and Spanish. So
I can talk to a lot of the boys. It is just the
English players I can't speak to at the moment!"

CHANGING LEAGUES
"It is different everywhere I go – the culture,
the football, everything. I have played for
big clubs in Germany and Spain but the fans
see football differently in England.

ENGLISH FOOTBALL
"The atmosphere all around the stadiums is
really fantastic. On the pitch the players show
great spirit and play a lot quicker. It suits me.
The Premier League is the best league in the
world. The fans are incredible."

IT'S A FACT!

• He cost City £4.7m when he
arrived from Atletico Madrid in
July 2007.
• As well as Bulgaria, he'd also
played in Switzerland, Germany
and Spain before England.
• He was banned for six
games after being sent off
for elbowing an opponent in
an Under-18 tournament.

POSITION: Striker
BORN: August 13, 1978, Bulawayo, Zimbabwe
PREVIOUS CLUBS: Jomo Cosmos, Grasshoppers (loan), Auxerre, Portsmouth
FACT: Benjani cost City £3.87m from Portsmouth and he scored on his first start for them – in the 2-1 victory over arch-rivals Man United!

BENJANI MWARUWARI

POSITION: Striker
BORN: October 24, 1985, Liverpool
PREVIOUS CLUBS: Everton
FACT: Wayne's younger brother, John, plays for Macclesfield and his cousin, Tommy Amos, is on the books at Wigan.

WAYNE ROONEY

MAN UNITED The Red Devils

SEASON 2007-08

PREMIER LEAGUE: Champions
FA CUP: Semi-final,
Man United 0 Portsmouth 1
LEAGUE CUP: Third round,
Man United 0 Coventry 2
EUROPE: Champions League winners,
Man United 1 Chelsea 1 (aet, United
won 6-5 on penalties)
HIGH POINT: It has to be capturing Fergie's
second European Cup.
LOW POINT: Losing both derby games against
bitter local rivals Man City.

PLAYER OF THE SEASON

Could there really be anyone other
than **CRISTIANO RONALDO**? Forget the
one-trick pony and diving accusations, this
was the season
the Portugal star
became a global
phenomenon.
Skill, tricks, speed
and goalscoring
ability made him
a massive threat
and earned him
both the PFA and
Football Writers
Player of the Year
awards. He was
also the Premier
League's top
scorer!

STAR PLAYER: OWEN HARGREAVES

POSITION: Midfielder **BORN:** January 20, 1981,
Calgary, Canada **TRANSFER VALUE:** £16m

HIS TIME AT BAYERN MUNICH
"The tension in the team at times at Bayern was
probably a bit too much. There were tackles and
fights all the time. At Munich you are expected
to know your place and it is very difficult for
a young player to break through in Germany."

OLD TRAFFORD HOPES
"We can win anything we enter because of
the strength of our squad and the age of the
players. We've got talented younger players
but also older experienced ones like
Ryan Giggs, Paul Scholes and Edwin
van der Sar."

LEAST FAVOURITE GROUND?
"Anfield. No rival fans want you to win
but Liverpool have very passionate
supporters and it's funny to hear the
things they shout at you."

MOST DIFFICULT OPPONENTS
"Kaka and Juninho. It's difficult to completely
knock these top players out of the game."

BEST PLAYER EVER
"Zinedine Zidane. A complete player
with strenth and amazing vision."

BOSS FERGIE SAYS
"There are a variety of roles Owen
can play. He has the intelligence and application
to adapt. Playing for England against Portugal
he was driving forward throughout the game
and getting beyond their midfield."

IT'S A FACT!

• Owen's eldest brother,
Darren, has played for Canada
at Youth level.
• His Dad, Colin, was on the
books at Bolton Wanderers
before emigrating to Canada.

• Fans voted him England's Player
of the Year in 2006 for his World
Cup campaign performances.
• Hargo was 19 when he made
his first-team debut for Bayern
Munich.

MIDDLESBROUGH
The Boro

SEASON 2007-08

PREMIER LEAGUE: 13th
FA CUP: Quarter-final, Boro 0 Cardiff 2
LEAGUE CUP: Third round, Spurs 2 Boro 0
EUROPE: n/a
HIGH POINT: Beating Arsenal 2-1 at the Riverside, the Gunners' first league defeat in eight months.
LOW POINT: Losing 3-2 at rivals Sunderland to a 92nd-minute own-goal!

PLAYER OF THE SEASON

Pipped by Stewart Downing for the Fans' Player of the Year, central defender **DAVID WHEATER** got the Young Player of the Year award. His outstanding form last term led to the sale of Jonathan Woodgate and earned the local youngster a deal to 2012. The imposing centre half, who has a knack of scoring goals, also earned a call up to the full England squad.

STAR PLAYER STEWART DOWNING

POSITION: Winger **BORN:** July 22, 1984, Middlesbrough **TRANSFER VALUE:** £14m

FIRST ENGLAND CALL-UP
"I sort of knew I was going to get picked the day before the team came out because [manager] Steve McClaren hinted to me I might be included. Then it was just a case of sitting and watching the television to get confirmation."

ENGLAND FORM
"People have talked to me about being the natural left-footed midfielder that England have been missing, they've said I could be the answer, but it's not really happened for me yet."

MEMORABILIA
"I'm a bit of a hoarder and have always kept everything to do with my career. The FA sent me a letter to say congratulations on my England call-up and listing all of the training camps. It is alongside all the other football memorabilia I've got."

SIGNING A NEW DEAL
"It was nice to get it out of the way so that I can just concentrate on playing my game. The chairman and the

manager have never pressurised me, they just made it clear that they wanted me to stay. It's not just about playing for my hometown club, I want to win something, and to do that with Boro would be the best."

FAVOURITE PLAYER
"Last season [2007], Ronaldo was probably the best player in the Premier League. This year, no one even gets close. Playing United is always difficult, but playing them with Ronaldo is a whole new ball game."

IT'S A FACT!

• He scored three goals in just seven games whilst on loan at north east rivals Sunderland.
• Stewart runs a charity in honour of his sister, Vicki, who died from leukaemia at the age of four in 1993.
• Boro gave one of their best-ever contracts to keep him at the club until 2013.

AFONSO ALVES

POSITION: Striker
BORN: January 30, 1981,
Belo Horizonte, Brazil
PREVIOUS CLUBS: Atletico Mineiro,
Orgryte, Malmo, Heerenveen
FACT: Boro's record buy at £12.7m
hit seven goals in Heerenveen's 9-0 victory
over Heracles in October 2007.

OBAFEMI MARTINS

POSITION: Striker
BORN: October 28, 1984, Lagos, Nigeria
PREVIOUS CLUBS: Inter Milan
FACT: Although many fans thought his £10m transfer fee was a lot of cash, Oba has proved a bargain buy – especially as Newcastle have only had to pay the money in installments.

NEWCASTLE UNITED

NEWCASTLE
The Magpies

SEASON 2007-08

PREMIER LEAGUE: 12th
FA CUP: Fourth round, Arsenal 3 Newcastle 0
LEAGUE CUP: Third round, Arsenal 2 Newcastle 0
EUROPE: Inter Toto winners
HIGH POINT: Winning 4-1 at Tottenham after falling behind.
LOW POINT: The crushing 5-1 home defeat to champions Manchester United after a 6-0 drubbing at Old Trafford.

PLAYER OF THE SEASON

HABIB BEYE, the Senegal right back, got off to a quiet start after being bought from Marseille by former boss Sam Allardyce. But he quickly found his feet and won over fans with his determination, work rate, desire to get forward and some great crosses. The fact he's said he wants to stay at St. James' Park will have won over the doubters.

STAR PLAYER: STEVEN TAYLOR

POSITION: Defender **BORN:** January 23, 1986, Greenwich, London **TRANSFER VALUE:** £8m

TYNE-WEAR DERBIES
"The two games you look for when the fixtures come out are the matches with Sunderland. You don't need a team talk if you know what it means to the fans. As soon as you cross that white line you know exactly what a derby match means. You don't want to lose."

EQUALISING AGAINST ARSENAL
"It was my first Premiership goal at St. James' Park and I dedicated it to the fans. There's no better feeling than seeing the ball go in."

JOINING THE TOON
"It wasn't that long ago that it was me on the terraces – in the Sir John Hall Stand – and now I am training with my heroes. It really is unbelievable. Alan Shearer was my Newcastle hero when I was young and I have trained with him."

HIS SHIRT NUMBER
"It came from when Philippe Albert was here, he was my idol. Then Jonathan

Woodgate came in and got the number 27. When he left I asked Sir Bobby Robson and he gave me the number. Now it's a big task to follow those two legends."

BOSS KEEGAN SAYS
"I like Steven Taylor. I think he has got leadership qualities in the making. I have been very impressed with him every time I have seen him play for a long time now."

IT'S A FACT!

• Despite where he was born – his father's job took him to London – Tayls is regarded as a Geordie.
• He has skippered England Under-21s and had one full England squad call last season.

• Tayls joined Newcastle as a nine-year-old and has always been a member of the Toon Army.
• He played for Wallsend Boys, the club that also produced Carrick, Shearer and Beardsley.

PORTSMOUTH Pompey

SEASON 2007-08

PREMIER LEAGUE: 8th
FA CUP: Winners, Portsmouth 1 Cardiff City 2
LEAGUE CUP: Fourth round, Portsmouth 1 Blackburn 2
EUROPE: n/a
HIGH POINT: Reaching the FA Cup Final for the first time in 69 years and lifting the trophy.
LOW POINT: Just two away wins from January until the end of the season ended hopes of a higher finish.

PLAYER OF THE SEASON

Defender **GLEN JOHNSON** caught the eye of new England boss Fabio Capello and was certainly one of Pompey's stars last term. There were a lot of candidates for Player of the Season, but the right-back topped the charts for most-improved. The former West Ham man, who failed to find his feet at Chelsea, appears to be a player reborn thanks to the help of Harry Redknapp. Still just 24.

STAR PLAYER: DAVID JAMES

POSITION: Goalkeeper **BORN:** August 1, 1970, Watford, Hertfordshire, **TRANSFER VALUE:** £1.5m

CRITICISM
"I don't like getting criticised because ultimately I have pride in my performances. If you'd have asked me how I felt when I was at Liverpool and getting called 'Calamity James', I honestly could not see a future for myself."

STRIKERS
"They have songs sung about them at Fratton Park. Mine is 'England's No.1'. That's it! I don't have the most rhythmic name for a song!"

AFTER WORK
"I have a lot of time when I am not playing. The modern footballer doesn't go out, or maybe I am the unsociable footballer. There was a time when I liked to go nightclubbing, but not anymore. I still like music but I don't DJ."

PREPARING FOR GAMES
"I think about everything. Part of my preparation is going over games and videos, looking at goals, good, bad and indifferent and analysing what I have done wrong and work on it."

JOINING POMPEY
"It was a big decision as I knew this would probably be the last move of my career. My mum said she enjoyed Portsmouth. I wouldn't want to upset her! I have found a Starbucks café, so I am happy."

BOSS HARRY REDKNAPP SAYS
"He is the best trainer I have ever seen. He is absolutely fantastic and will go on to play until he is 42 if he wants."

IT'S A FACT!
- He used to read the dictionary to learn more words.
- He is an energy conservationist and switches off lights at home. His car also runs on rapeseed oil!
- He earned an England recall at the age of 37!
- Jamo is a keen artist who takes commissions for pictures and sells his work.

JERMAIN DEFOE

POSITION: Striker
BORN: Beckton, East London, October 7, 1982
PREVIOUS CLUBS: West Ham, Spurs
FACT: He kick-started his Hammers career by hitting 19 goals in just 31 games during a loan spell at Bournemouth. That included a record ten goals in ten consecutive matches.

POSITION: Midfielder
BORN: December 14, 1981, Retford, Nottinghamshire
PREVIOUS CLUBS: Mansfield, Sunderland
FACT: The Republic of Ireland star has twice been promoted to the Premiership, having helped Sunderland go up in 2005.

LIAM LAWRENCE

STOKE CITY
The Potters

SEASON 2007-08

CHAMPIONSHIP: 2nd
FA CUP: Third round,
Newcastle 4 Stoke 1 (replay)
LEAGUE CUP: First round, Rochdale 2 Stoke 2
(aet, Stoke lost 4-2 on pens)
EUROPE: n/a
HIGH POINT: Going on a 12-game unbeaten
run between November and January.
LOW POINT: Losing captain Andy Griffin to
injury in April after persuading him to return
to the club during the transfer window.

PLAYER OF THE SEASON

LIAM LAWRENCE, the former Sunderland
midfielder, picked up three pieces of
silverware at the club's Player of the Year
Awards and added another from supporters.
He was also the Potters' most efficient player
according to Actim Stats, helped by his
14 goals.

STAR PLAYER: RYAN SHAWCROSS

POSITION: Defender **BORN:** October 4, 1987,
Chester **TRANSFER VALUE:** £2m

LEAVING MAN UNITED
"My contract there was up in the summer
[2007] and Sir Alex wanted me to stay. It was
very hard to leave, though, as they made me
a very good offer."

WHY STOKE?
"Sir Alex told me that if I was going to go to
one club, it should be Stoke. The attraction
of playing first-team football every week here
was what swayed my decision."

PLAYER IDOL
"John Terry's the main one, he's a tough
defender. I used to model myself on
Rio Ferdinand but he's too good on the
ball for me!"

RESERVES V FIRST TEAM
"Playing against 16 and 17-year-olds in the
reserve league doesn't really improve your
game. Now I'm playing against men every
week and it's 100 miles per hour. This really
does toughen you up."

BOSS TONY PULIS SAYS
"I think Ryan's attitude and
approach to work and to
becoming a better player will
make him even better. He's still got a long
way to go before he's the finished article,
but there's no question he can get there at
his current rate of progress."

IT'S A FACT!
• Although he was raised in
Wales, Ryan is an England
Under-21 player.
• Ryan cost £1m when he moved
from Man United but is now
worth quite a bit more!
• Last December he agreed
a new deal until 2011.
• He hit seven goals in 27 games
whilst on loan from United.

SUNDERLAND
The Black Cats

SEASON 2007-08

PREMIER LEAGUE: 15th
FA CUP: Third round, Sunderland 0 Wigan 3
LEAGUE CUP: Second round, Luton 3 Sunderland 0
EUROPE: n/a
HIGH POINT: Winning their first away game of the season on March 22, against Aston Villa. The only goal, seven minutes from time by Michael Chopra, also gave them their first victory at Villa Park since 1982.
LOW POINT: The 4-0 home defeat against Man United, former club of boss Roy Keane.

PLAYER OF THE SEASON

Many football followers questioned Roy Keane's decision to buy striker **KENWYNE JONES** from Southampton. Stern John was allowed to move the other way in August 2007 as part of a deal worth around £6m for the Trinidad and Tobago hitman. Jones has proved a real handful for Premier League defenders with his height and power. His form led to him being linked with Chelsea and Liverpool.

STAR PLAYER: CRAIG GORDON

POSITION: Goalkeeper **BORN:** December 31, 1982, Edinburgh **TRANSFER VALUE:** £9m

PREMIER LEAGUE
"There are an awful lot of international players and I think that's the style of football that's played more in the Premiership than in Scotland. As I've played a lot of international football I think that helped me settle."

BEING SUCCESSFUL
"If you don't play to the best of your abilities you're going to get beaten in this division, no matter who you are playing against. You can't afford to have an off day and expect to still win."

HIS FORM
"I think I've done okay and I've been quite happy, but you have to keep proving yourself and it's the next game that's important."

BEING A BLACK CAT
"Everything's done for the players. The training ground has fantastic facilities, the hotels and the food and everything else is all organised and sorted so all you have to do is concentrate on your football."

MANAGER ROY KEANE
"It's always difficult coming to a different set-up with different ideas. He's been very good with everything he's done. It wasn't too long ago that he was a player himself so he understands."

BOSS KEANE SAYS
"Craig is a top goalkeeper and he'll be a massive asset to us over the next few years. He is a big signing for Sunderland."

IT'S A FACT!
- Craig played for boyhood heroes Hearts before moving to Sunderland.
- His transfer fee could rise to a total of £9m, a record for a British keeper.
- Father David was also a keeper, who turned out for teams in the lower Scottish leagues.
- The Scotland star turned down Aston Villa because he was impressed with Cats' boss Keano.

KENWYNE
JONES

POSITION: Central defender
BORN: January 22, 1980, Middlesbrough
PREVIOUS CLUBS: Leeds, Newcastle, Real Madrid, Middlesbrough
FACT: His first goal for Spurs was the extra-time League Cup winner against capital rivals Chelsea.

JONATHAN WOODGATE

TOTTENHAM *Spurs*

SEASON 2007-08

PREMIER LEAGUE: 11th
FA CUP: Fourth round, Man United 3 Spurs 1
LEAGUE CUP: Winners,
Tottenham 2 Chelsea 1 (aet)
EUROPE: UEFA Cup last 16, PSV 1 Spurs 1
(two legs, lost 6-5 on pens aet)
HIGH POINT: Winning the League Cup,
thrashing Arsenal 5-1 along the way.
LOW POINT: Hammered 4-1 at home to
Newcastle, the Geordies completing a double.

PLAYER OF THE SEASON

ROBBIE KEANE is just loved by the White Hart
Lane faithful. Not hard to see why in a year in
which the Republic of Ireland captain passed
the 100 goals milestone for the club, went
past 250 appearances for them and set a new
personal best for goals in a season with 23.

STAR PLAYER: JAMIE O'HARA

POSITION: Midfielder **BORN:** September 25,
1986, Dartford, Kent **TRANSFER VALUE:** £2.5m

MAKING A MARK
"Fans love to see a young English player coming
through. Top clubs have got the money to go out
and buy a player when they need one, so you
have to look at yourself and think: 'I want to be
that player.' Others will always come in so you
have to keep proving to the manager that you
can be part of his plans."

STAYING A SPUR
"The boss is building a squad that is going to be
up there challenging for honours and
to be told that I am part of his long-
term plans by giving me a three-year
deal is good for me. I have always
wanted to play for Spurs."

GOING OUT ON LOAN
"I would recommend it to any young
player. You have to go out and play
first-team football."

FAVOURITE PLAYER
"I've always wanted to be like Paul Scholes, a

central midfielder who scores
goals and runs games. I have watched
the way he dominates games – that's
what I want to achieve. I got his shirt
when we played them in the FA Cup."

BOSS JUANDE RAMOS SAYS
"Jamie has earned his time on the pitch. He
has come a long way in a short space of time.
If he continues in the same vein he will become
a very important player for us."

IT'S A FACT!

• He was the club's young Player
of the Season and supporters'
most promising youngster.
• Jamie has agreed a contract
extension to keep him at the
club until 2011.

• The new England Under-21
player trained with Tottenham's
arch-rivals Arsenal when he
was younger.
• He boosted his experience with
loans to Chesterfield and Millwall.

WEST BROM
The Baggies

CHAMPIONSHIP: Champions
FA CUP: Semi-finals, WBA 0 Portsmouth 1
LEAGUE CUP: Third round, WBA 2 Cardiff 4
EUROPE: n/a
HIGH POINT: Drawing at home to Southampton to clinch promotion.
LOW POINT: Playing as well as, if not better than, Portsmouth and losing the FA Cup semi-final.

PLAYER OF THE SEASON

Veteran striker **KEVIN PHILLIPS** grabbed the supporters' Player of the Year award for his 24 goals in 36 appearances. But then departed to second city rivals Birmingham!

STAR PLAYER JONATHAN GREENING

POSITION: Midfielder **BORN:** January 2, 1979, Scarborough **TRANSFER VALUE:** £2m

HIS FUTURE
"I fully intend to see out my contract because the boss has made that big an impact on me. I would like to end my career here. I have been here more than four years and I've got three years left and then as long as the gaffer wants me, I'd like to stay."

TONY MOWBRAY
"The gaffer is a top man. Everyone knows he's not all smiles when he's doing interviews but around the place he is always whistling and is a happy-go-lucky guy. Everyone loves training sessions with him and the way he likes to play. We know he's not a misery guts."

BEING SKIPPER
"Getting the captain's armband off him was a complete shock. I've thoroughly enjoyed it and working closely with the gaffer. The captaincy has probably helped my game this year, being a bit more organised and having more responsibility."

ROY KEANE
"I played with him a few times at Man United. He was a great player and great captain but I don't smash players up in the changing room like he did! He was always quite nice to me, probably because I was a young boy."

IT'S A FACT!

• Jonno began his career at York City and Man United but really made a name for himself at Middlesbrough.
• His mum texted him before the final game of the season to say he would win the Championship!
• He has 17 England Under-21 caps but has never made the full international side.
• Greening began all West Brom's league matches last term.

POSITION: Striker
BORN: March 5, 1987, Manchester
PREVIOUS CLUBS: Manchester City
FACT: Miller joined the Baggies on a season-long loan in August 2007 but during the January 2008 transfer window signed permanently in a £1.4m deal.

ISHMAEL MILLER

DEAN ASHTON

POSITION: Striker
BORN: November 24, 1983, Swindon
PREVIOUS CLUBS: Crewe, Norwich
FACT: He was West Ham's record signing when he moved from Norwich for £7.25m in 2006.

WEST HAM
The Hammers

SEASON 2007-08

PREMIER LEAGUE: 10th
FA CUP: Third round,
Man City 1 West Ham 0 (replay)
LEAGUE CUP: Quarter-finals,
West Ham 1 Everton 2
EUROPE: n/a
HIGH POINT: Bouncing back from one down to beat champions Man United 2-1 at Upton Park.
LOW POINT: Being without a host of injured star players for most of the season.

PLAYER OF THE SEASON

Hammer of the Year **ROB GREEN** has had two great seasons and was ever-present during the last campaign. It's a big surprise to a lot of football fans that he hasn't had more recognition from England but the keeper admits that he would never turn his back on his country if they come calling.

STAR PLAYER: MARK NOBLE

POSITION: Midfielder **BORN:** May 8, 1987, Canning Town, East London **TRANSFER VALUE:** £8m

BEST POSITION
"Central midfield is where I think I can really do my best. I'll give my best wherever the gaffer picks me, but centre midfield is always where I've played and it's the position I feel most comfortable in."

GROWING UP
"My school days were fantastic. I loved having the teacher come in during the lesson, on an afternoon, and say: 'Can he be excused, we've got a match to play?' I couldn't let my mates down but from 15 on it was just West Ham."

FIRST TEAM DEBUT
"My girlfriend came and watched me but my mum and dad were on holiday in Cyprus. They had no idea I was going to play but I think I did okay."

HOME GAMES
"It's scary. There's a great noise, a great occasion. It makes you do things you didn't realise you could do. When that West Ham crowd sings *Bubbles* and you hear 35,000 people – one voice all singing the same song. It makes me shiver."

BOSS ALAN CURBISHLEY SAYS
"Mark Noble's is the biggest-selling shirt in the club shop because he's home-grown. The fans have a great affinity with him and he displays all the qualities they want to see. There is plenty more to come from him."

IT'S A FACT!
• Mark's family always have a bet on him to score the first goal in a match.
• He was the youngest player to appear in the Hammers' reserves, aged 15. He was the fans' Young Player of the Year in 2006-07.
• Mark is proud of his East End roots and claims to be a big fan of pie and mash!

WIGAN ATHLETIC The Latics

SEASON 2007-08

PREMIER LEAGUE: 14th
FA CUP: Fourth round, Wigan 1 Chelsea 2
LEAGUE CUP: Second round, Wigan 0 Hull 1
EUROPE: n/a
HIGH POINT: The return of manager Steve Bruce in November to lift them away from relegation danger.
LOW POINT: An eight-game run of defeats between September and November.

PLAYER OF THE SEASON

Austrian **PAUL SCHARNER** can be relied on for an all-action display with some crunching tackles in both defence and midfield. He also weighed in with five goals from his 39 appearances during 2007-08 making him the clear winner of the supporters' Player of the Year Award.

STAR PLAYER KEVIN KILBANE

POSITION: Midfielder **BORN:** February 1, 1977, Preston **TRANSFER VALUE:** £1m

FIGHTING RELEGATION

"You are looking over your shoulder. You see the other fixtures that teams have. Where they might slip up, where they might pick up points. But you just have to get on and do your own job."

RUMOURS OF LEAVING WIGAN

"To be honest, I felt comfortable all season. Earlier in the season there were rumours about a lot of players leaving and going to different clubs. But I didn't feel there would be a time when I would be moving on."

IRELAND'S NEW MANAGER

"Giovanni Trapattoni Is a big name and one we are all going to be looking forward to working under. He is going to bring in different ideas and methods and I am sure every player who takes part will look forward to it."

BOSS STEVE BRUCE SAYS

"The one thing about him is

that he is a top-class professional who never moans or groans. He just gets on with it. That's why he's had the career he's had because he is one of those Steady Eddies who anybody would welcome in their dressing room."

IT'S A FACT!

- Kilbane was the Republic of Ireland's Player of the Year in 2005.
- His brother Farrell plays in the Conference North.
- Kevin became West Brom's first £1m player when they bought him from Preston North End in 1997.
- Kilbane has also played for Sunderland and Everton and should pass the 90 cap mark for Ireland.

POSITION: Striker
BORN: January 11, 1978, Leicester
PREVIOUS CLUBS: Leicester City, Liverpool, Birmingham City
FACT: The England striker cost Liverpool a club record £11m when he joined them from Leicester in 2000.

WIGAN ATHLETIC

EMILE HESKEY

THE CHAMPIONSHIP

AMAZING FACTS, STUNNING STATS AND INSIDE INFORMATION ON THE CLUBS WHO CURRENTLY FORM ENGLAND'S SECOND-BEST LEAGUE

READING

2007-08 PREMIER LEAGUE POSITION: 18th, relegated
FA CUP: Third round, lost 1-0 to Spurs (replay)
LEAGUE CUP: Third round, lost 4-2 to Liverpool

DID YOU KNOW?
If Reading had netted four more times last season they would still be in the Premiership! The Royals were relegated courtesy of an inferior goal difference to lucky survivors Fulham. Manager Steve Coppell's men gave it a real go in the final game of the season, recording a 4-0 victory over bottom side Derby – 8-0 was a bit much to ask!

WACKY FACT
Royals' winger John Oster beat multiple World Champion Phil "The Power" Taylor 2-0 during a darts charity event.

BIRMINGHAM CITY

2007-08 PREMIER LEAGUE POSITION: 19th, relegated
FA CUP: Third round, lost 2-1 to Huddersfield Town
LEAGUE CUP: Third round, lost 3-0 to Blackburn

DID YOU KNOW?
Mikael Forssell grabbed City's only hat-trick in the Premier League last season during the Blues' 4-1 win over Spurs at St. Andrews. The Finland striker hit goals in the 7th, 59th and 81st minutes. He was the joint 20th highest-scorer in the Premiership with Aston Villa's Gareth Barry, Boro's Stewart Downing and Newcastle's Obafemi Martins.

WACKY FACT
Stopper Colin Doyle was the joint ninth tallest player in the Premiership last season at 196cm (6ft 5in).

DERBY COUNTY

2007-08 PREMIER LEAGUE POSITION: 20th, relegated
FA CUP: Fourth round, lost 4-1 to Preston North End
LEAGUE CUP: Second round, lost on penalties to Blackpool

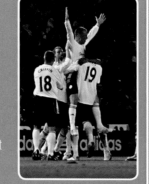

DID YOU KNOW?
The Rams won just one league game during 2007-08 – against Newcastle at Pride Park. Kenny Miller netted in the 39th minute and Derby hung on. Unfortunately that was as good as it got for the Derbyshire outfit. The Rams were unbeaten against the Magpies all year – one of their eight draws also came against Newcastle at St. James' Park!

WACKY FACT
Derby's Jack Stamps burst the ball with a shot during the 1946 FA Cup Final! Stamps looked to have sealed victory with a fierce strike which beat Charlton keeper Sam Bartram – but was deflated when the ball punctured, denying him the glory. Derby won 4-1.

BRISTOL CITY

2007-08 CHAMPIONSHIP POSITION: 4th
FA CUP: Third round, lost 2-1 to Middlesbrough
LEAGUE CUP: Second round, lost 2-1 to Manchester City

DID YOU KNOW?
Bristol City beat Hull in their last Championship meeting during the regular season before losing out to them in the play-off final at Wembley. In March 2008 the Robins won 2-1 at home, with strikes from Dele Adebola and Jamie McCombe. Two months later Hull progressed to the top-flight when a Dean Windass volley beat the West Country side.

WACKY FACT
Famous City fans include BBC commentator Jonathan Pearce, Tony Robinson – also known as "Baldrick" from the *Blackadder* television series – and England cricket star Marcus Trescothick.

CRYSTAL PALACE

2007-08 CHAMPIONSHIP POSITION: 5th
FA CUP: Third round, lost 2-0 to Watford
LEAGUE CUP: First round, lost on penalties to Bristol Rovers

DID YOU KNOW?
The Eagles' biggest win of the 2007-08 Championship came in their final game of the regular season. Victory was needed to ensure a place in the play-offs and strikes from Ben Watson, Victor Moses, Tom Soares, Scott Sinclair and Clinton Morrison saw the Selhurst Park outfit sign-off with a 5-0 demolition of Burnley. Palace lost out to Bristol City in the play-off semi-finals.

WACKY FACT
In 1973 the club crest was changed to feature an eagle – hence the club's nickname. It was suggested that the "eagle" should resemble a phoenix, reflecting the fact that the club had lived on even though its original home at Crystal Palace burned to the ground in the 1930s.

WATFORD

2007-08 CHAMPIONSHIP POSITION: 6th
FA CUP: Fourth round, lost 4-1 to Wolverhampton Wanderers
LEAGUE CUP: Second round, lost 2-0 to Southend United

DID YOU KNOW?
Watford went top of the Championship on February 9, 2008, when they beat Ipswich 2-1 at Portman Road. Another win followed against Leicester and automatic promotion looked likely. Then the Hornets had a horrendous run which saw them claim just one win in 14 games. They lost 6-1 on aggregate to Hull City in the play-off semi-finals.

WACKY FACT
Legendary rock star Sir Elton John used to be chairman of the Hornets. A fan since the age of seven Sir Elton took the job back in 1976. Apparently, members of the 1978 squad sang vocals on Elton's *A Single Man* album! He remains honorary life president.

WOLVES

2007-08 CHAMPIONSHIP POSITION: 7th
FA CUP: Fifth round, lost 2-0 to Cardiff
LEAGUE CUP: Second round, lost 3-1 to Morecambe

DID YOU KNOW?
Not only was Sylvan Ebanks-Blake Wolves' top goal-scorer last season, netting 12 times in just 20 appearances – he was the hottest striker in the Championship. He arrived at Molineux during the January 2008 transfer window having bagged 13 goals for Plymouth earlier in the season! The 22-year-old began his career at Manchester United for whom he made two appearances in the League Cup.

WACKY FACT
When the club formed in 1877, it was as a schoolboys' team called St. Luke's FC. Apparently the club's founders, John Baynton and Jack Brodie, presented a football as a prize for a group of hardworking pupils. Two years later St. Luke's merged with the local football and cricket club – the Wanderers – and Wolverhampton Wanderers were born. Wolves were a founder member of the Football League in 1888.

IPSWICH TOWN

2007-08 CHAMPIONSHIP POSITION: 8th
FA CUP: Third round, lost 1-0 to Portsmouth
LEAGUE CUP: First round, lost to MK Dons after penalties

DID YOU KNOW?
Ipswich drew 15 games during the campaign. Converting just one of those into a victory would have seen the East Anglian side into the play-offs. In their first away game of the season Ipswich gave away an equalising penalty in the 85th minute against Plymouth!

WACKY FACT
When Ipswich beat Bristol City 6-0 in the league last season they were just one goal away from equalling their best-ever league victory. The Blues defeated Portsmouth 7-0 during an old Division 2 encounter back in November 1964. Incidentally, Ipswich's worst league loss came against Fulham – they were thrashed 10-1 in Division 1 on December 26, 1963.

SHEFFIELD UNITED

2007-08 CHAMPIONSHIP POSITION: 9th
FA CUP: Fifth round, lost 1-0 after extra time in replay to Middlesbrough
LEAGUE CUP: Fourth round, lost 3-0 to Arsenal

DID YOU KNOW?
Sheffield United kept 15 clean sheets during 2007-08 – the only club to record more games without conceding a goal were Wolves (19) and Leicester (17). In February the Blades went 270 minutes without letting a goal in – but they didn't score any either during 0-0 draws against Scunthorpe (Championship), West Brom (Championship) and Middlesbrough (FA Cup). Defender Chris Morgan ended Sheffield's goal drought in the 78th minute of their next game against QPR.

WACKY FACT
Sheffield United own a club in China called Chengdu Blades. United bought the then-named Chengdu Five Bulls in 2006. The Chinese team also wear red and white.

PLYMOUTH ARGYLE

2007-08 CHAMPIONSHIP POSITION: 10th
FA CUP: Fourth round, lost 2-1 to Portsmouth
LEAGUE CUP: Third round, lost 1-0 to West Ham

DID YOU KNOW?
The first player to score for Plymouth in the Championship last season was David Norris after just 15 minutes of the Pilgrims' clash against Hull City. But that wasn't the first goal of the game – Dean Windass had put Hull ahead in the third minute. Plymouth won 3-2 but midfielder Norris has since moved to Ipswich Town.

WACKY FACT
Paul Sturrock is the 39th manager of Plymouth Argyle since the club formed more than 100 years ago. Famous names to have led the Pilgrims include former England keeper Peter Shilton and ex-Northern Ireland player and manager Billy Bingham. Sturrock took over at the end of 2007 but the Scot had been gaffer at Argyle before. He led the Pilgrims from 2000 to 2004, guiding them to victory in the Football Third Division during 2001-02.

CHARLTON ATHLETIC

2007-08 CHAMPIONSHIP POSITION: 11th
FA CUP: Third round, lost 4-3 on penalties after 2-2 replay to West Brom
LEAGUE CUP: Third round, lost 3-1 to Luton

DID YOU KNOW?
Charlton fielded 38 different players in the Championship last season, the same number as Southampton, QPR and Crystal Palace. Only Leicester put more players into action – a total of 41.

Keeper Nicky Weaver made the most league appearances for the Addicks in 2007-08, playing 45 games out of 46! He was sent off at Plymouth, preventing him from completing a clean sweep.

WACKY FACT
Charlton fans sing a song called *Valley, Floyd Road* to the tune of Paul McCartney's *Mull of Kintyre*. One of the verses goes "From Selhurst to West Ham, Many years did we roam, Forever dreaming of returning home" in reference to the Addicks' longed-for return to The Valley. They had been forced to leave the ground in the mid-1980s due to financial difficulties. They played their first game back at the new Valley on December 5, 1992.

CARDIFF CITY

2007-08 CHAMPIONSHIP POSITION: 12th
FA CUP: Final, lost 1-0 to Portsmouth
LEAGUE CUP: Fourth round, lost 2-1 to Liverpool

DID YOU KNOW?
Cardiff had their fair share of ageing stars last season. At 36-years-old, Jimmy Floyd Hasselbaink made 33 appearances in the league, netting on seven occasions. Robbie Fowler, 33, bagged four from ten games while 35-year-old midfielder Trevor Sinclair played 14 times and scored once.

WACKY FACT
Mascots Bartley the Bluebird and, more recently, Bartley Blue, are apparently named after Bartley Wilson, the first secretary of the club in its original incarnation as Riverside FC. Wilson played a big part in forming a football club from players at Riverside Cricket Club back in 1899. After merging with Riverside Albion in 1902, the club became Cardiff City in 1908.

BURNLEY

2007-08 CHAMPIONSHIP POSITION: 13th
FA CUP: Third round, lost 2-0 to Arsenal
LEAGUE CUP: Third round, lost 1-0 to Portsmouth

DID YOU KNOW?

The highest attendance at Turf Moor during 2007-08 was 16,843 when the Clarets hosted local rivals Blackpool in a 1-1 draw. Burnley's lowest attendance was 9,779 against Coventry City in February.

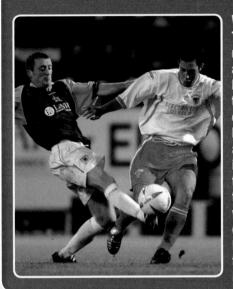

WACKY FACT

The Clarets hosted nearly 17,000 against Blackpool last term – but that's nothing compared with the highest attendance at Turf Moor. Back in 1924, 54,775 fans squeezed into the ground to watch them take on Yorkshire rivals Huddersfield in the third round of the FA Cup.

QUEENS PARK RANGERS

2007-08 CHAMPIONSHIP POSITION: 14th
FA CUP: Third round, lost 1-0 to Chelsea
LEAGUE CUP: First round, lost 2-1 to Leyton Orient

DID YOU KNOW?

Dexter Blackstock scored the final goal of QPR's 2007-08 Championship season in the 15th minute of their 1-0 win over Charlton. Unfortunately there were two more games to play and the Hoops failed to net against either Norwich or West Brom. Blackstock was the joint fourth highest scorer for the Loftus Road side last term with six goals, while the hottest striker award went to Akos Buzsaky who converted ten times.

WACKY FACT

When the Hoops first formed the only equipment they had were four goalposts and two lengths of tape for crossbars! Actually, QPR played in light and dark blue halves on their shirts to start with. It was only in 1892 that the "hoops" design was used – although they were green and white! By 1927 Rangers had swapped kit again for the distinctive blue and white hoop shirt.

PRESTON NORTH END

2007-08 CHAMPIONSHIP POSITION: 15th
FA CUP: Fifth round, lost 1-0 to Portsmouth
LEAGUE CUP: First round, lost 2-1 to Morecambe

DID YOU KNOW?

Preston scored 50 goals in the Championship last season – 12 fewer than bottom-placed Colchester! Neil Mellor bagged nine for the Lilywhites but the next-highest goalscorer was Chris Brown with five. Colchester's Kevin Lisbie, on the other hand, netted on 17 occasions during the league and three other players had seven or more. Unfortunately for United they conceded 86 during 2007-08 compared with Preston's 56!

WACKY FACT

North End's most famous player, Tom Finney, was known as "The Preston Plumber". Despite having played 473 times for the Lilywhites and earned 76 caps for England, the legendary winger

returned to the plumbing trade when he retired from football. In 2004, Sir Tom unveiled a water feature sculpture outside the ground that relives a famous image of the winger that won the 1956 Sports Photograph of the Year.

SHEFFIELD WEDNESDAY

2007-08 CHAMPIONSHIP POSITION: 16th
FA CUP: Third round, lost 4-2 on penalties after 1-1 replay to Derby
LEAGUE CUP: Third round, lost 3-0 to Everton

DID YOU KNOW?

Wednesday recorded a win and a draw against neighbours Sheffield United in the league last season. Goals from Akpo Sodje and Marcus Tudgay at Hillsborough gave the Owls a 2-0 victory during January, while a brace from Adam Bolder was enough for a point against the Blades at Bramall Lane three months later. During the course of the clubs' histories United have 41 league wins in the local derby compared with the Owls' 33.

WACKY FACT

In 1887 Wednesday players earned five shillings (25p) for home games and seven shillings and sixpence (37.5p) for away games! The club was formed in 1867 by members of Wednesday Cricket Club – the "Wednesday" part of the name refers to the only half day of the week the players had off work!

NORWICH CITY

2007-08 CHAMPIONSHIP POSITION: 17th
FA CUP: Third round, lost 2-1 in replay to Bury
LEAGUE CUP: Third round, lost 1-0 to Manchester City

DID YOU KNOW?
Jamie Cureton was their only player to bag a hat-trick during the 2007-08 League campaign. The 32-year-old netted three times in the Canaries 5-1 win against his former club Colchester. Cureton finished the season as the club's top scorer on 12 goals.

WACKY FACT
The Canaries' kit for their UEFA Cup tie against Bayern Munich came seventh in an online list of worst ever shirts. Described as the "paintball" or "bird poo" shirt, it was a mind-blowing mass of green and yellow. Norwich beat Bayern in Germany and drew at Carrow Road to make it into the third round against Inter Milan in 1993.

BARNSLEY

2007-08 CHAMPIONSHIP POSITION: 18th
FA CUP: Semi-final, lost 1-0 to Cardiff City
LEAGUE CUP: Second round, lost 2-0 to Newcastle United

DID YOU KNOW?
Official statistics show Barnsley had 241 shots on target last term. Unfortunately, they also had 243 that were wide of the mark! Compare these stats with league champions West Brom who aimed successfully between the sticks 385 times. Colchester had the worst shooting record with just 192 useful attempts.

WACKY FACT
Tune into 1575AM and on match days you'll get Barnsley's very own radio station. The studios at Oakwell have broadcast every home game since the station was launched in 1996.

BLACKPOOL

2007-08 CHAMPIONSHIP POSITION: 19th
FA CUP: Third round, lost 2-1 to Barnsley
LEAGUE CUP: Fourth round, lost 2-0 to Tottenham

DID YOU KNOW?
Blackpool had the second-best disciplinary record in the Championship last season. The Tangerines committed just 475 fouls, compared with Coventry City's 642, and received only 48 yellow and four red cards (Coventry had 90 and four!) in cup football. The only team to be better behaved was Colchester United— but they were relegated!

WACKY FACT
According to the club's website, mascot Bloomfield Bear's claim to fame is that he has danced with 1990s chart-toppers Steps. His favourite food is crackers with apple jam and peanut butter and his ambition is to lead the Tangerines out in an FA Cup Final at Wembley!

SOUTHAMPTON

2007-08 CHAMPIONSHIP POSITION: 20th
FA CUP: Fifth round, lost 1-0 to Bristol Rovers
LEAGUE CUP: First round, lost 2-1 to Peterborough

DID YOU KNOW?
Stern John left it until the 69th minute of the final game of last season to secure Southampton's Championship future for 2008-09. Level at 2-2 with Sheffield United, John bagged his second goal of the game with just over 20 minutes to go but left the St. Mary's fans biting their nails when he was sent off for a second bookable offence ten minutes from the end.

WACKY FACT
The Saints aren't the only football club with a religious-themed nickname. Woking are known as the Cardinals, York City are Minstermen, Boston United and Plymouth Argyle are both called the Pilgrims and Darlington are the Quakers!

COVENTRY CITY

2007-08 CHAMPIONSHIP POSITION: 21st
FA CUP: Fifth round, lost 5-0 to West Brom
LEAGUE CUP: Fourth round, lost 2-1 to West Ham

DID YOU KNOW?
The son of legendary Manchester United and Denmark keeper Peter Schmeichel played nine games for Coventry last term. Kasper Schmeichel joined the Sky Blues on loan from Manchester City in March, and helped the Ricoh Arena side secure their place in the Championship.

WACKY FACT
There is an elephant on the club's badge. The animal – similar to the one that appears on the City of Coventry's own coat of arms – is balancing on a blue and white football while carrying a castle on its back! The elephant was introduced to the club crest in the early 1960s when veteran TV presenter Jimmy Hill was manager.

SWANSEA CITY

2007-08 LEAGUE 1 POSITION: Champions
FA CUP: Third round, lost 4-2 in replay to Havant & Waterlooville
LEAGUE CUP: Second round, lost 1-0 to Reading after extra time

DID YOU KNOW?
Swansea finished ten points clear of Nottingham Forest at the top of League 1 last season to earn promotion. The Welsh side lost just eight games, winning 27 and drawing 11 to amass 92 points. Much of the credit must go to forward Jason Scotland, the division's top scorer with 24 goals.

WACKY FACT
Three sets of brothers played for the Swans during their 1953-54 season in the old Second Division – Cyril and Gilbert Beech, Cliff and Bryn Jones and Ivor and Len Allchurch. Southampton fielded three brothers – Danny, Rod and Ray Wallace – in the First Division back in 1988.

NOTTINGHAM FOREST

2007-08 LEAGUE 1 POSITION: 2nd
FA CUP: Second round, lost 1-0 to Luton Town
LEAGUE CUP: Second round, lost 3-2 to Leicester City

DID YOU KNOW?
Forest kept 24 clean sheets in the league – seven more than champions Swansea City. Keeper Paul Smith played in every one of Forest's 46 league games last term. In April 2008, Smith kept the ball out of the net for 316 consecutive minutes – that's over five hours! Yeovil's Jaime Peters ended that run in the 20th minute of Forest's final game of the season.

WACKY FACT
Nottingham Forest were the first club to use shinpads – back in 1874. Four years later a referee used a whistle for the first time during Forest's game against Sheffield Norfolk. And Forest apparently invented the 2-3-5 formation of two full-backs, three half-backs and five forwards!

DONCASTER ROVERS

2007-08 LEAGUE 1 POSITION: 3rd, promoted through play-offs
FA CUP: First round, lost 2-1 in replay to Oldham Athletic
LEAGUE CUP: Second round, lost 2-0 to Plymouth

DID YOU KNOW?
Doncaster's 1-0 play-off final victory over Leeds lifted them into the second tier of English football for the first time in more than 50 years. Rovers were agonisingly close to securing automatic promotion but a 2-1 loss to Cheltenham on the final day meant a tense play-off campaign. After comprehensively beating Southend in the semis, it was a James Hayter header against Leeds that took Doncaster to the Championship.

WACKY FACT?
Former Doncaster player Chris Balderstone is one of the few sportsmen to have played professional football and cricket – at the same time! On one occasion in 1975 he batted all afternoon for Leicestershire before heading off to play for Rovers at 7.30pm that same evening! He returned to the cricket ground the following day to complete his century and finish with bowling figures of 3 for 28!

LEICESTER CITY

2007-08 CHAMPIONSHIP POSITION: 22nd, relegated
LEAGUE CUP: Fourth round, lost 4-3 to Charlton
JOHNSTON'S PAINT TROPHY: Did not play
HIGH: A Matty Fryatt strike gave the Foxes a shock 1-0 victory over Premiership Aston Villa in the third round of the League Cup.
LOW: Needing a victory on the final day of the season, Leicester drew 0-0 and were relegated to the third tier of English football.

SCUNTHORPE UNITED

2007-08 CHAMPIONSHIP POSITION: 23rd, relegated
LEAGUE CUP: First round, lost 2-1 to Hartlepool
JOHNSTONE'S PAINT TROPHY: Did not play
HIGH: Scunthorpe bagged 20 points from the first 14 games last season – the sort of form that should have seen them avoid the drop.
LOW: A 5-0 pummelling at the hands of West Brom during an appalling run that saw United win just one game in 17.

COLCHESTER UNITED

2007-08 CHAMPIONSHIP POSITION: 24th, relegated
LEAGUE CUP: First round, lost 1-0 to Shrewsbury
JOHNSTONE'S PAINT TROPHY: Did not play
HIGH: A 3-0 win over Preston in Colchester's third game of the season followed two draws and things looked bright.
LOW: United won just seven games in 46, and suffered a 5-1 thrashing from Coventry City.

CARLISLE UNITED

2007-08 LEAGUE 1 POSITION: 4th
LEAGUE CUP: Second round, lost 2-0 to Coventry
JOHNSTONE'S PAINT TROPHY: Northern quarter-finals, lost 3-0 to Stockport
HIGH: A 3-0 win over Leyton Orient mid-season in the middle of a run of 12 games without a defeat.
LOW: Defeat in the play-off semi-finals to Leeds United.

LEEDS UNITED

2007-08 LEAGUE 1 POSITION: 5th
LEAGUE CUP: Second round, lost 3-0 to Portsmouth
JOHNSTONE'S PAINT TROPHY: Northern Section quarter-finals, lost 2-1 to Bury
HIGH: A 3-2 aggregate win over Carlisle in the play-off semi-finals took United to Wembley
LOW: A 15-point deduction by the Football League meant Leeds were always going to be up against it – defeat to Doncaster in the play-off final finished them off.

SOUTHEND UNITED

2007-08 LEAGUE 1 POSITION: 6th
LEAGUE CUP: Third round, lost 2-1 to Blackpool (aet)
JOHNSTONE'S PAINT TROPHY: First round, lost on penalties to Dagenham & Redbridge.
HIGH: Consecutive wins over Swindon Town, Walsall, Crewe and Brighton at the end of the season.
LOW: A 5-1 defeat to Doncaster in the play-off semi-final second leg.

BRIGHTON

2007-08 LEAGUE 1 POSITION: 7th
LEAGUE CUP: First round, lost 1-0 to Cardiff City
JOHNSTONE'S PAINT TROPHY: Southern semi-finals, lost 1-0 to Swansea City
HIGH: Six goals and six points from two games (against Southend and Millwall) early in the season showed plenty of promise.
LOW: Failing to reach the Johnston's Paint regional final.

OLDHAM ATHLETIC

2007-08 LEAGUE 1 POSITION: 8th
LEAGUE CUP: 2nd round, lost 3-0 to Burnley
JOHNSTONE'S PAINT TROPHY: 2nd round, lost 3-0 to Doncaster
HIGH: Beating Everton 1-0 at Goodison Park in the third round of the FA Cup with a spectacular 25-yard strike from Gary McDonald.
LOW: After winning their opening game, the Latics suffered five consecutive League defeats.

NORTHAMPTON TOWN

2007-08 LEAGUE 1 POSITION: 9th
LEAGUE CUP: Second round, lost 2-0 to Middlesbrough
JOHNSTONE'S PAINT TROPHY: First round, lost 2-0 to Luton
HIGH: A 4-2 revenge victory (see below) over eventual League 1 champions Swansea near the end of the campaign.
LOW: A 3-0 defeat at the hands of Swansea City in the run-up to Christmas.

HUDDERSFIELD TOWN

2007-08 LEAGUE 1 POSITION: 10th
LEAGUE CUP: First round, lost 1-0 to Blackpool
JOHNSTONE'S PAINT TROPHY: First round, lost 4-1 to Grimsby
HIGH: A 1-0 home victory against Leeds in front of their biggest crowd of the season – 16,413!
LOW: Losing 4-1 to Southend and then 4-0 to neighbours Leeds United within the space of three days.

TRANMERE ROVERS

2007-08 LEAGUE 1 POSITION: 11th
LEAGUE CUP: First round, lost 1-0 to Stockport County
JOHNSTONE'S PAINT TROPHY: First round, lost 1-0 to Morecambe
HIGH: After losing their first game of the season Rovers went on a ten-game unbeaten league run.
LOW: Four defeats in the last five games.

WALSALL

2007-08 LEAGUE 1 POSITION: 12th
LEAGUE CUP: First round, lost 2-0 to Swansea
JOHNSTONE'S PAINT TROPHY: First round, lost 2-0 to Bournemouth
HIGH: After a poor start Walsall bagged consecutive wins against Hartlepool and Doncaster before recording their biggest victory of the campaign – a 4-0 thrashing of Huddersfield
LOW: Two points from the first five League games.

SWINDON TOWN

2007-08 LEAGUE 1 POSITION: 13th
LEAGUE CUP: First round, lost 2-0 to Charlton
JOHNSTONE'S PAINT TROPHY: Second round, lost 3-1 to Cheltenham
HIGH: An impressive 6-0 victory over Port Vale in April.
LOW: A heartbreaking replay defeat on penalties to League 2 Barnet in the FA Cup.

LEYTON ORIENT

2007-08 LEAGUE 1 POSITION: 14th
LEAGUE CUP: Second round, lost 1-0 to Cardiff City
JOHNSTONE'S PAINT TROPHY: Second round, lost 1-0 to Dagenham & Redbridge
HIGH: After a poor run of results Orient signed off with a 3-1 home win over Bristol Rovers.
LOW: A 3-1 defeat at Gillingham was followed by a 5-0 thrashing at the hands of Swansea City.

HARTLEPOOL

2007-08 LEAGUE 1 POSITION: 15th
LEAGUE CUP: Second round, lost 2-1 to Sheffield Wednesday (aet)
JOHNSTONE'S PAINT TROPHY: Northern quarter-finals, lost on penalties to Morecambe
HIGH: Snatching all three points with a 3-2 victory over Port Vale, courtesy of two goals in the last three minutes.
LOW: Two points from their final six games of the season.

BRISTOL ROVERS

2007-08 LEAGUE 1 POSITION: 16th
LEAGUE CUP: Second round, lost 2-1 to West Ham
JOHNSTONE'S PAINT TROPHY: Second round, lost 1-0 to Bournemouth
HIGH: Reaching the FA Cup quarter-finals by beating Southampton 1-0.
LOW: After losing the final three games of the 2007-08 season Rovers finished just five points clear of relegation.

MILLWALL

2007-08 LEAGUE 1 POSITION: 17th
LEAGUE CUP: First round, lost 2-0 to Northampton
JOHNSTONE'S PAINT TROPHY: First round, lost 3-2 to Swansea
HIGH: Beating Carlisle 3-0 at home in the second to last game of the season, securing their League 1 status.
LOW: A 4-0 thrashing at Carlisle.

YEOVIL TOWN

2007-08 LEAGUE 1 POSITION: 18th
LEAGUE CUP: 1st round, lost 4-1 to Hereford
JOHNSTONE'S PAINT TROPHY: Southern quarter-finals, lost 1-0 Swansea
HIGH: Ten points from their first five League games.
LOW: Two successive 3-0 defeats – at Oldham and home to Southend.

CHELTENHAM TOWN

2007-08 LEAGUE 1 POSITION: 19th
LEAGUE CUP: First round, lost 4-1 to Southend
JOHNSTONE'S PAINT TROPHY: Southern quarter-finals, lost 4-1 to Brighton
HIGH: Paul Connor's 85th-minute winner in the final game confirmed Town were safe from relegation.
LOW: Four consecutive defeats prior to their last game.

CREWE ALEXANDRA

2007-08 LEAGUE 1 POSITION: 20th
LEAGUE CUP: First round, lost 3-0 to Hull City
JOHNSTONE'S PAINT TROPHY: First round, lost on penalties to Chester
HIGH: Six goals in two games in March – during a 3-0 win at Gillingham and 3-1 against Hartlepool.
LOW: Looking for a win on the final day of the season to ensure survival, Crewe went down 4-1 to Oldham. Results elsewhere went in their favour.

MK DONS

2007-08 LEAGUE 2 POSITION: Champions – promoted
LEAGUE CUP: Second round, lost 3-2 to Sheffield United (aet)
JOHNSTONE'S PAINT TROPHY: Champions, beat Grimsby 2-0
HIGH: A 3-2 victory at Stockport ensured Paul Ince's men promotion – and they won the JP Trophy at Wembley too!
LOW: Dons took just four points from their first five League 2 games!

PETERBOROUGH UNITED

2007-08 LEAGUE 2 POSITION: 2nd – promoted
LEAGUE CUP: Second round, lost 2-0 to West Bromwich Albion
JOHNSTONE'S PAINT TROPHY: Second round, lost 3-1 to MK Dons
HIGH: Following a superb end-of-season run, a 1-0 win at Hereford United saw Peterborough promoted.
LOW: Two League Two defeats in a row followed by an exit from the League Cup back in August 2007 was as bad as it got.

HEREFORD UNITED

2007-08 LEAGUE 2 POSITION: 3rd – promoted
LEAGUE CUP: Second round, lost 2-1 to Birmingham City
JOHNSTONE'S PAINT TROPHY: Second round, lost on pens to Yeovil
HIGH: A 3-0 win at Brentford in the second-to-last game of the campaign saw Hereford climb into League 1.
LOW: Going down 4-0 at Chesterfield in January put a dent in an otherwise successful campaign.

STOCKPORT COUNTY

2007-08 LEAGUE 2 POSITION: 4th – play-off winners
LEAGUE CUP: Second round, lost 4-3 to Charlton
JOHNSTONE'S PAINT TROPHY: Northern semi-finals, lost 2-1 to Grimsby
HIGH: Goals from Anthony Pilkington and Liam Dickinson secured a Wembley play-off final victory for County over local rivals Rochdale.
LOW: A 4-0 loss at Darlington was a low point in the quest for promotion.

ALL YOU NEED TO KNOW ABOUT... LEAGUE TWO

BOURNEMOUTH

2007-08 LEAGUE 1 POSITION: 21st – relegated
LEAGUE CUP: First round, lost 1-0 to West Bromwich Albion
JOHNSTONE'S PAINT TROPHY: Southern Section quarter-finals, lost 2-0 to MK Dons
HIGH: Winning six of their last seven League 1 games – but it wasn't quite enough!
LOW: Having ten points deducted for going into administration.

GILLINGHAM

2007-2008 LEAGUE 1 POSITION: 22nd – relegated
LEAGUE CUP: First round, lost 3-0 to Watford
JOHNSTONE'S PAINT TROPHY: Southern Section semi-finals, lost to MK Dons on penalties
HIGH: Being within six minutes of a place in the Johnstone's Paint Southern final.
LOW: Losing 4-0 to Nottingham Forest and 5-0 to Swindon in 14 days.

PORT VALE

2007-2008 LEAGUE 1 POSITION: 23rd – relegated
LEAGUE CUP: First round, lost to Wrexham on penalties
JOHNSTONE'S PAINT TROPHY: Second round, lost to Morecambe on penalties
HIGH: A 3-0 win against Cheltenham in October 2007 looked like it could put the Robins' season back on track.
LOW: Conceding five first-half goals in a 6-0 loss to Swindon.

LUTON TOWN

2007-2008 LEAGUE 1 POSITION: 24th – relegated
LEAGUE CUP: Fourth round, lost 1-0 to Everton
JOHNSTONE'S PAINT TROPHY: Second round, lost 4-3 to Gillingham
HIGH: Winning their first two games of the season – Hartlepool in the League and Dagenham & Redbridge in the Carling Cup.
LOW: Finishing bottom and being relegated for the second successive season.

ROCHDALE

2007-2008 LEAGUE 2 POSITION: 5th
LEAGUE CUP: Second round, lost to Norwich City on penalties
JOHNSTONE'S PAINT TROPHY: 2nd round – lost 3-1 to Bury
HIGH: Beating Darlington on penalties to reach the play-off final.
LOW: Losing 3-2 to Stockport at Wembley in that final.

DARLINGTON

2007-2008 LEAGUE 2 POSITION: 6th
LEAGUE CUP: First round, lost 2-1 to Barnsley
JOHNSTONE'S PAINT TROPHY: Second round, lost 1-0 to Leeds
HIGH: Going top of League 2 after a 3-0 away win at Accrington Stanley
LOW: Agonisingly missing out on a play-off final at Wembley after losing on penalties to Rochdale.

WYCOMBE WANDERERS

2007-2008 LEAGUE 2 POSITION: 7th
LEAGUE CUP: First round, lost 2-1 to Plymouth Argyle
JOHNSTONE'S PAINT TROPHY: Second round, lost 2-0 to Swansea
HIGH: Leading Stockport 1-0 in the first leg of the play-off semis, courtesy of a Delroy Facey strike.
LOW: Scoring two own goals during a 6-0 League defeat against Stockport – the side that put them out in the play-offs!

CHESTERFIELD

2007-2008 LEAGUE 2 POSITION: 8th
LEAGUE CUP: First round, lost 3-1 to Sheffield United
JOHNSTONE'S PAINT TROPHY: First round, lost 3-1 to Hartlepool
HIGH: A 4-0 win at Wrexham at the start of a seven-game unbeaten run mid-season.
LOW: A 1-1 draw with Darlington ended hopes of a play-off place.

ROTHERHAM UNITED

2007-2008 LEAGUE 2 POSITION: 9th
LEAGUE CUP: First round, lost 3-1 to Sheffield Wednesday
JOHNSTONE'S PAINT TROPHY: Second round, lost to Grimsby on penalties
HIGH: Winning the final four games of the season – against Grimsby, Dagenham & Redbridge, Mansfield Town and Barnet.
LOW: Losses of 4-1 (Rochdale) and 5-1 (Morecambe) followed by the lowest crowd of the season at Millmoor – 2,979 v Brentford.

BRADFORD CITY

2007-2008 LEAGUE 2 POSITION: 10th
LEAGUE CUP: First round, lost 2-1 to Wolves
JOHNSTONE'S PAINT TROPHY: First round, lost 5-1 to Doncaster
HIGH: Two wins in four days against Chester City – in the League and then the FA Cup – immediately after a devastating run of bad form (see below).
LOW: An appalling run that comprised five consecutive losses followed by two draws and another loss – that's two points from eight games!

MORECAMBE

2007-2008 LEAGUE 2 POSITION: 11th
LEAGUE CUP: Third round, lost 5-0 to Sheffield United
JOHNSTONE'S PAINT TROPHY: Northern Section Final, lost 1-0 (agg) to Grimsby
HIGH: Beating Lancashire rivals Bury to reach the JP Trophy Northern Final.
LOW: Three games in succession without a goal against Grimsby – Morecambe lost to them in the league and then over two legs in the JP Trophy Northern Final.

BARNET

2007-2008 LEAGUE 2 POSITION: 12th
LEAGUE CUP: 1st round – lost 5-2 to Norwich City
JOHNSTONE'S PAINT TROPHY: 2nd round – lost 2-1 to Brighton
HIGH: Four wins on the spin - against Chesterfield, Rotherham, Wycombe and Stockport – during September and October.
LOW: Barnet scored just one goal in 450 minutes of League football during the month of February.

BURY

2007-2008 LEAGUE 2 POSITION: 13th
LEAGUE CUP: First round, lost 1-0 to Carlisle
JOHNSTONE'S PAINT TROPHY: Northern Section semi-finals, lost 2-0 to Morecambe
HIGH: Beating Championship side Norwich City 2-1 in an FA Cup third round replay.
LOW: A 5-1 defeat at the hands of MK Dons.

BRENTFORD

2007-2008 LEAGUE 2 POSITION: 14th
LEAGUE CUP: First round, lost 3-0 to Bristol City
JOHNSTONE'S PAINT TROPHY: First round, lost 4-1 to Swindon
HIGH: A nine-game unbeaten streak that included seven wins after Christmas 2007.
LOW: A 7-0 thrashing at Peterborough – it all went wrong when Bees' keeper Simon Brown was sent off in the second minute!

LINCOLN CITY

2007-2008 LEAGUE 2 POSITION: 15th
LEAGUE CUP: First round, lost 4-1 to Doncaster
JOHNSTONE'S PAINT TROPHY: Second round, lost 5-2 to Hartlepool
HIGH: An amazing five League wins in 14 days during February – against Shrewsbury, Macclesfield, Rochdale, Accrington Stanley and Macclesfield.
LOW: Conceding eight goals during the first two games of the season – 4-0 to Shrewsbury in the league and 4-1 to Doncaster in the League Cup.

GRIMSBY TOWN

2007-2008 LEAGUE 2 POSITION: 16th
LEAGUE CUP: First round, lost to Burnley on penalties
JOHNSTONE'S PAINT TROPHY: Final, lost 2-0 to MK Dons
HIGH: Beating Morecambe over two legs to reach the Johnstone's Paint Final.
LOW: Town endured a miserable finish to the League season, losing their last seven games.

ACCRINGTON STANLEY

2007-2008 LEAGUE 2 POSITION: 17th
LEAGUE CUP: First round, lost 1-0 to Leicester
JOHNSTONE'S PAINT TROPHY: First round, lost 3-2 to Oldham
HIGH: Coming off the back of four consecutive losses (including an 8-2 drubbing at Peterborough), Stanley's Ian Craney netted in the 90th minute at Chester to secure three priceless points.
LOW: Going out of the League Cup and JP Trophy in the first round – then losing 3-2 to Huddersfield in their FA Cup opener.

SHREWSBURY TOWN

2007-2008 LEAGUE 2 POSITION: 18th
LEAGUE CUP: Second round, lost 1-0 to Fulham
JOHNSTONE'S PAINT TROPHY: First round, lost 1-0 to Yeovil
HIGH: A 4-0 win on the first day of the season at Lincoln City.
LOW: Shrewsbury's 1-1 draw at Morecambe in April 2008 represented the Shropshire side's 15th game in a row without a victory.

MACCLESFIELD TOWN

2007-2008 LEAGUE 2 POSITION: 19th
LEAGUE CUP: First round, lost 1-0 to Leeds
JOHNSTONE'S PAINT TROPHY: Second round, lost 1-0 to Stockport
HIGH: A 1-0 win over Peterborough in January ended a nine-game run without a victory.
LOW: A 5-0 loss to Mansfield Town (who would go on to be relegated) confirmed things weren't going well for Macclesfield!

DAGENHAM & REDBRIDGE

2007-2008 LEAGUE 2 POSITION: 20th
LEAGUE CUP: First round, lost 2-1 to Luton
JOHNSTONE'S PAINT TROPHY: Southern Section quarter-finals, lost 4-0 to Gillingham
HIGH: Winning their last two games (against Darlington and Mansfield Town) bodes well for this year's League 2 campaign.
LOW: Losing 4-0 to Chester in their third game of the season (having picked up one point from their two openers) wasn't a good omen.

NOTTS COUNTY

2007-2008 LEAGUE 2 POSITION: 21st
LEAGUE CUP: 1st round, lost 3-0 to Coventry
JOHNSTONE'S PAINT TROPHY: 1st round, lost 1-0 to Leyton Orient
HIGH: A 1-0 victory over Wycombe Wanderers courtesy of a Richard Butcher strike ended County's relegation worries for the season.
LOW: Drawing for the fourth game in a row at Stockport in February. The Magpies drew more games than any club (18) during a frustrating season.

CHESTER CITY

2007-2008 LEAGUE 2 POSITION: 22nd
LEAGUE CUP: First round, lost to Nottingham Forest on penalties
JOHNSTONE'S PAINT TROPHY: Second round, lost 4-2 to Carlisle
HIGH: A draw and two wins to kick off the season – including a 4-0 victory over Dagenham & Redbridge.
LOW: Chester failed to score in each of the last four games of the season.

ALDERSHOT TOWN

2007-2008 BLUE SQUARE PREMIER POSITION: 1st – promoted
LEAGUE CUP: Did not play
JOHNSTONE'S PAINT TROPHY: Did not play
HIGH: Finishing a staggering 15 points clear at the top of the Blue Square Premier to earn automatic promotion.
LOW: "Only" managing to draw their final four games of the season!

EXETER CITY

2007-2008 BLUE SQUARE PREMIER POSITION: Fourth, promoted through play-offs
LEAGUE CUP: Did not play
JOHNSTONE'S PAINT TROPHY: Did not play
HIGH: Returning to the Football League following a five-year absence courtesy of a play-off final victory over Cambridge United.
LOW: A 4-0 away defeat to Kidderminster early in the season.

QUIZ ANSWERS

CROSSWORD P36-37
Across: 1. Valley
4. Savage 8. Dale
9. Osman 10. Cech
13. Iain 14. Parker
16. Hyypia 18. O'Neill
20. Celtic 22. Distin
26. Heskey 28. Owen
31. Neil 32. Eagle
33. Eto'o 34. Shorey
35. Stuart

Down: 2. Allardyce
3. Yossi 4. Shay 5. Greek
6. Edwin 7. Third
11. Diop 12. Bale
15. Gold 17. Arca
19. Leicester 21. Theo
23. Song 24. China
25. Kalou 27. Smith
29. Wales 30. Gary

KNOW YOUR FOOTBALL P44-45
Captains
1. William Gallas
2. Michael Owen
3. Steven Gerrard
4. John Terry
5. Kevin Nolan

Shirt numbers
a. Edwin van der Sar
b. Obafemi Martins
c. Emmanuel Adebayor
d. Peter Crouch
e. Andrew Johnson

Last season
1. Chelsea
2. West Brom
3. Cristiano Ronaldo
4. Fulham
5. Colchester

Which country?
1. Togo
2. Australia
3. Ghana
4. Senegal
5. Paraguay

Winners
a. FA Cup
b. Tottenham
c. Aldershot
d. Swansea City
c. SPL

CROSSWORD P50-51
Across: 1. Sami 3. Micah
6. Park 8. Dawson
9. Arteta 11. Evra 13.
Hleb 14. Riise 16. Stubbs
17. Adam 18. Tiger
19. Ball

20. Gareth 22. Pedro
23. Blue 24. Gera
27. Essien 29. Vieira
30. Seol 31. Scots
32. Nets

Down: 1. Sodje
2. Insua 3. Manchester
4. Claret 5. Huth 6. Pat
7. Keane 10. Aliadiere
12. Routledge
15. Hargreaves
21. Alonso 22. Pulis
24. Green 25. Adams
26. Hibs 28. Sol